Mrs New

CW00496261

Key Stage Two
Year 5 Maths

Homework Sheets

Photocopiable Worksheets for Differentiated Learning

About the Book

This book has homework sheets for all the topics in Year 5 Maths. It can also be used with the books for Years 3, 4 and 6 to make a complete homework scheme for Key Stage 2 Maths.

Each Sheet in a Topic is More Difficult than the Last

We've split the Framework up into topics such as 'Fractions' or 'Number Patterns'. Each sheet covers objectives from the Framework.

For the <u>first homework</u> on Written Adding and Subtracting, you'll set your class these sheets:

SUPPORT	Sheet 3
CORE	Sheet 4
EXTENSION	Sheet 5

For the <u>second set of homework</u> on Written Adding and Subtracting, you set your class these sheets:

SUPPORT	Sheet 4
CORE	Sheet 5
EXTENSION	Sheet 6

Objective Coverage is Shown at the Front of the Book

For each sheet of a topic, we've said what objective or part-objective is being covered.

EXAMPLE TOPIC

Topic name.

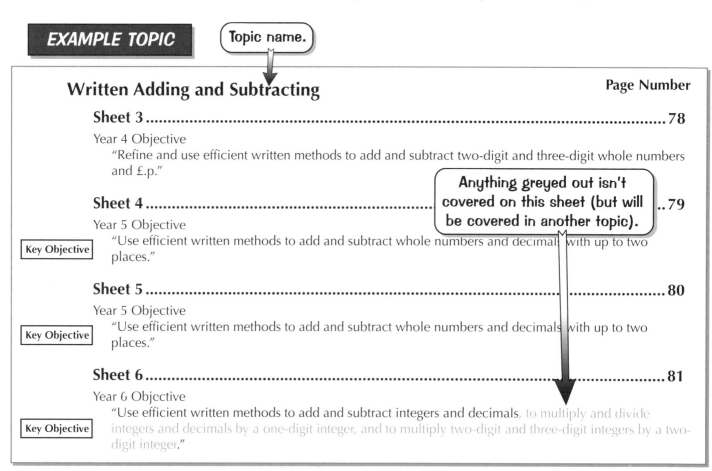

Online Resources

We've made a Resource Finder and Homework Tracker to help you use the Homework Sheets. They both have <u>tutorials</u> and are free. They're at <u>www.cgpbooks.co.uk/ks2maths</u>

Use the Resource Finder to Choose Homework Sheets

1. Select the school year and the <u>strand or block</u> you're teaching

2. Choose the <u>topic or objective</u> you need resources for.

3. It'll show you which Homework Sheets to use. It'll also suggest sheets for <u>support</u> and <u>extension</u> groups.

Don't worry, darling —
it's not really black and white.

Oh, Hank, thank you.
I was so terribly, terribly afraid.

First, choose how you want to search here.
Then, click on the bits you're teaching here.

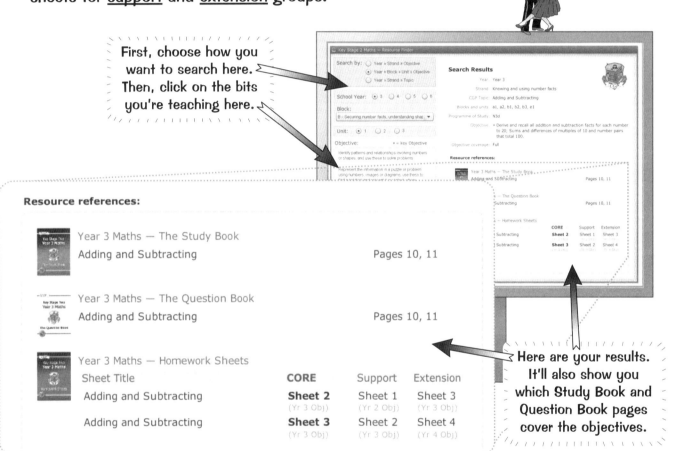

Resource references:

	Year 3 Maths — The Study Book	
	Adding and Subtracting	Pages 10, 11
	Year 3 Maths — The Question Book	
	Adding and Subtracting	Pages 10, 11

Year 3 Maths — Homework Sheets			
Sheet Title	**CORE**	Support	Extension
Adding and Subtracting	**Sheet 2** (Yr 3 Obj)	Sheet 1 (Yr 2 Obj)	Sheet 3 (Yr 3 Obj)
Adding and Subtracting	**Sheet 3** (Yr 3 Obj)	Sheet 2 (Yr 3 Obj)	Sheet 4 (Yr 4 Obj)

Here are your results. It'll also show you which Study Book and Question Book pages cover the objectives.

The Homework Tracker Records Each Pupil's Progress

The Homework Tracker is a spreadsheet. It'll help you <u>record which sheets each child has completed</u>, and <u>if they've achieved the objective</u>.

We've used <u>traffic light colour-coding</u> so you can see at a glance how well each child has done on the sheets. You can make sheets for individual pupils for use at <u>parents' evenings</u>.

At the end of the year, you can pass the spreadsheet on to the class's next teacher.

Published by Coordination Group Publications Ltd.

Editors:
Jane Aston, Joe Brazier, Katherine Craig, Charley Darbishire, Heather Gregson,
Sarah Hilton, Sharon Keeley, Luke von Kotze, Simon Little, Hannah Louise Nash,
Michael Southorn, Julie Wakeling.

Contributors:
Deborah Beattie, Emma Buckley, Stephanie Burton, Barbara Cartwright, Neil Davies,
Sue Foord, Adam Higgins, Joanne Kingston, Anita Loughrey, Amanda MacNaughton,
Chris Martin, Katy Servanté, Kim Sissons, Alyson Smith.

With thanks to Andrew Meller, Tina Ramsden, Glenn Rogers
and Laurence Stamford for the proofreading.

ISBN: 978 1 84762 188 7

Groovy website: www.cgpbooks.co.uk

Printed by Elanders Hindson Ltd, Newcastle upon Tyne.
Jolly bits of clipart from CorelDRAW®
Thumb illustration used throughout the book © iStockphoto.com

Text, design, layout and original illustrations © Coordination Group Publications Ltd. 2008
All rights reserved.

Objective Coverage

Section 1 — Using and Applying Mathematics

Explaining Problem Solving

Number Patterns

Page Number

Objective Coverage

Objective Coverage

Section 2 — Counting and Understanding Number

Objective Coverage

Decimals

Fractions

Objective Coverage

Key Objective

Objective Coverage

Proportion and Ratio

Year 4 Objective
> "Use the vocabulary of ratio and proportion to describe the relationship between two quantities (e.g. 'There are 2 red beads to every 3 blue beads, or 2 beads in every 5 beads are red'); estimate a proportion (e.g. 'About one quarter of the apples in the box are green')."

Year 5 Objective
> "Use sequences to scale numbers up or down; solve problems involving proportions of quantities (e.g. decrease quantities in a recipe designed to feed six people)."

Year 6 Objective
> "Solve simple problems involving direct proportion by scaling quantities up and down."

Rounding

Year 4 Objective
> "Partition, **round** and order **four-digit whole numbers**; use positive and negative numbers in context and position them on a number line; state inequalities using the symbols < and > (e.g. -3 > -5, -1 < +1)."

Year 5 Objective

Key Objective
> "Explain what each digit represents in whole number and decimals with up to two places, and partition and order these numbers; **round whole numbers and decimals with up to two places**."

Year 6 Objective
> "Use decimal notation for tenths, hundredths and thousandths; partition, **round** and order **decimals with up to three places**, and position them on the number line."

Objective Coverage

Section 3 — Knowing and Using Number Facts

Adding and Subtracting

Checking Calculations

Objective Coverage

Objective Coverage

Section 4 — Calculating

Calculators

Objective Coverage

Mental Maths

Multiply by 10, 100 and 1000

Objective Coverage

Using Fractions

Year 4 Objective
"Find fractions of numbers, quantities or shapes (e.g. 1/5 of 30 plums, 3/8 of a 6 by 4 rectangle)."

Year 5 Objective
"Find fractions using division (e.g. 1/100 of 5 kg), and percentages of numbers and quantities (e.g. 10%, 5% and 15% of £80)."

Year 6 Objective
"Relate fractions to multiplication and division (e.g. 6 ÷ 2 = 1/2 of 6 = 6 × 1/2); express a quotient as a fraction or decimal (e.g. 67 ÷ 5 = 13.4 or 13 2/5); find fractions and percentages of whole-number quantities (e.g. 5/8 of 96, 65% of £260)."

Written Adding and Subtracting

Year 4 Objective
"Refine and use efficient written methods to add and subtract two-digit and three-digit whole numbers and £.p."

Year 5 Objective
Key Objective
"Use efficient written methods to add and subtract whole numbers and decimals with up to two places."

Year 5 Objective
Key Objective
"Use efficient written methods to add and subtract whole numbers and decimals with up to two places."

Year 6 Objective
Key Objective
"Use efficient written methods to add and subtract integers and decimals, to multiply and divide integers and decimals by a one-digit integer, and to multiply two-digit and three-digit integers by a two-digit integer."

<u>*Objective Coverage*</u>

Written Multiplying and Dividing

Section 5 — Understanding Shape

2D Shapes

Objective Coverage

Key Objective

Objective Coverage

Objective Coverage

Drawing Shapes

Symmetry

Transformations

Objective Coverage

Section 6 — Measuring

Objective Coverage

Objective Coverage

Units and Measures Page Number

Section 7 — Handling Data

Analysing Data

Objective Coverage

Objective Coverage

Tables and Charts   **Page Number**

Year 4 Objective

Key Objective   "Answer a question by identifying what data to collect; organise, present, analyse and interpret the data in tables, diagrams, tally charts, pictograms and bar charts, using ICT where appropriate."

Year 4 Objective

"Compare the impact of representations where scales have intervals of differing step size."

Year 5 Objective

Key Objective   "Construct frequency tables, pictograms and bar and line graphs to represent the frequencies of events and changes over time."

Year 6 Objective

Key Objective   "Solve problems by collecting, selecting, processing, presenting and interpreting data, using ICT where appropriate; draw conclusions and identify further questions to ask."

Year 6 Objective

"Construct and interpret frequency tables, bar charts with grouped discrete data, and line graphs; interpret pie charts."

Explaining Problem Solving

1 | **Here are some signs:** | $+$ | $-$ | $\div$ | $=$ |

Use the signs to make these calculations correct:

a) $18\ \boxed{}\ 3 = 6$

b) $24\ \boxed{}\ 9 = 15$

c) $42\ \boxed{}\ 12\ \boxed{}\ 54$

2 | Grace has saved up £4.30 to buy a new basketball. Her mum gives her £2.45 more.

How much money does she have altogether? Show your working.

3 | **A sports shop has the following offers:**

Naseen wants to buy 6 tennis balls.
Which is the cheapest offer?
Explain your answer.

Offer 1

3 Packs for the Price of 2

Offer 2

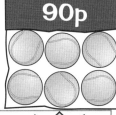
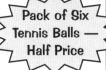

Pack of Six Tennis Balls — Half Price

Activity | Write a <u>word problem</u> that could be solved using the calculation 7×4.

Fool.

Learning Objective:

"I can explain to someone else how I solved a problem or puzzle."

© 2008 CGP

Explaining Problem Solving

1 There are 3 different types of chocolate in a jar. Rosie takes out a chocolate without looking.

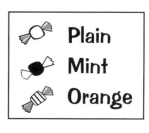

Plain
Mint
Orange

   a)   Which chocolate is Rosie most likely to pull out? Explain how you know.

   b)   Rosie puts the chocolate back and adds three more orange chocolates to the jar. Which type is she most likely to pull out now? Explain why.

2 **25 is a square number.**

Draw a diagram to explain how you know this.

A square number is found by multiplying another number by itself.

3 A garden centre sells square concrete slabs like this: Romina buys 6 square concrete slabs for her patio.

4 m
4 m

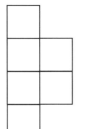

She lays the slabs in the pattern shown. What is the perimeter of Romina's patio? Show your working.

Activity   Zach rolls two dice (numbered 1 to 6). Write down all the number combinations that he could have rolled for the following scores:

3   5   6   8   10   11   12

Learning Objective:

"I can write down how I solved a problem, showing every step."

SHEET 4

© 2008 CGP

Explaining Problem Solving

1 Isaac thinks of a 2 digit number. It is a multiple of 7.
It ends in 2. The sum of its digits is 6.

What is the number? ☐

Explain how you know.

---

2 Look at this puzzle grid:

Each shape represents a number. The totals of
each row and column are shown.

a)   Work out the values of ☐, ▲ and ⬤

▲	⬤	☐	⬤	17
▲	⬤	▲	⬤	16
▲	☐	⬤	☐	16
▲	▲	☐	☐	14
12	17	16	18	

b)   Which shape value did you work out first? Explain why you did this.

Activity   Kyle and his friends go to the cinema.
A small popcorn costs £1.20. A large popcorn costs £1.60.
They buy at least one of each size and spend exactly £8.00.
Work out how many of each popcorn size they bought.

Learning Objective:

"I can explain to someone else how I
solved a problem or puzzle."

© 2008 CGP

Explaining Problem Solving

1 | Look at this sorting diagram:

a) Put these numbers in the
correct place on the diagram:
4 6 7 8 9 18

b) Lewis says '36 is a square number
so it will have an odd number of
factors.' Explain why Lewis is correct.

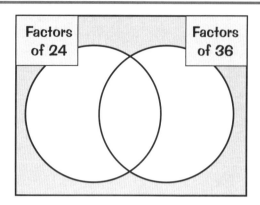

Remember — factors usually come in pairs of different numbers.

2 | Year 5 and Year 6 have a choice of either pasta or curry for school dinner.

Altogether there are 89 children
in Year 5 and Year 6. 21 Year 5
children choose pasta. Use this to work
out the missing numbers in the table.

	Curry	Pasta	Total
Year 5			47
Year 6		19	
Total			

3 | Eddie goes to his favourite fast food restaurant.

2 cheeseburgers and 1 portion of chips costs £3.80
1 hotdog and 1 portion of chips costs £2.00
1 portion of chips and 1 cheeseburger costs £2.30

How much does each item of food cost? Show your working.

Activity   Scarlett sits at a table with her friends Davina,
Adam and Greg. Scarlett does not change her
seat. How many ways can Scarlett's friends sit?

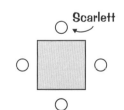

Scarlett

Learning Objective:

"I can write down how I solved a
problem, showing every step."

    © 2008 CGP

Explaining Problem Solving

1 | Ellie thinks of a number. She halves the number, then multiplies it by 10. Her answer is 330.

What number did she start with? Show your method.

2 | This spinner is divided into 8 equal sections.

Asid says 'There is a greater chance of an even number coming up than an odd number.'

Do you agree? Yes [ ] No [ ]

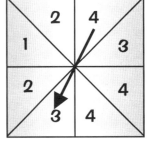

Explain your answer.

3 | Look at this sequence: 42 32 22 12 2 ...

a) Lauren says 'Every negative number in the sequence will end in 8.'
Explain why Lauren is correct.

b) What is the first negative number in the sequence below -100?
Explain how you know.

Activity | I have a 10p coin, a 2p coin, a 5p coin and a 20p coin in a bag.
I pull out 2 coins. Record all the amounts I could have made.

Learning Objective:

"I can show how I solved a problem, explaining every step."

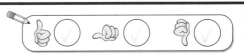

6 Name: .... Date: ....

Number Patterns

1 | Fill in the missing numbers and work out the rule: |

a) 32   36   40   ☐ ☐ ☐   The rule is ☐

b) 450 400 350   ☐ ☐ ☐   The rule is ☐

c) ☐ ☐ ☐ ☐   80 100 120 The rule is ☐

2 | Alex has some numbered cards: |

 ☐2☐ ☐3☐ ☐4☐ ☐7☐

Use the cards to make 2 sums where the answers are <u>odd</u> numbers.

a) ☐ ☐ **+** ☐ ☐   b) ☐ ☐ **+** ☐ ☐

c) Complete the rule by circling the correct word in each box:

Odd / Even **+** Odd / Even **=** Odd Number

3 | Grid A is a pattern on your classroom window. |

In Grid B draw how the pattern would look from the other side of the glass.

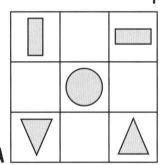

Grid A   Grid B

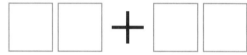
Use the line of reflection to help.

| **Activity** | You need to make <u>less than 20p</u> using <u>only 2 coins</u>. Record the different <u>amounts</u> and which <u>coins</u> you have used.

Learning Objective:

"I can identify patterns between numbers and test them with my own examples."

SHEET 4   © 2008 CGP

Number Patterns

1 | Complete the sequence and work out the rule: |

a) 63　51　☐　☐　☐　☐　　The rule is ☐

b) 80　105　☐　☐　☐　☐　　The rule is ☐

c) 3　6　12　☐　☐　☐　　The rule is ☐

2 | Jane says "Any number ending in **28** will always be divisible by **4**." |

Do you agree with Jane?　Explain your answer.

☐

3 | I think of a number.　I multiply it by **2** and add **7**.　My answer is **31**. |

What was my original number?　Remember to show your working.

☐

4 | Katie draws two shapes. |

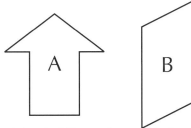

a)　True or False?

Shape A is a hexagon. ☐

Shape B has **2** pairs of parallel lines. ☐

b)　Write a true statement about the angles in Shape A.

☐

c)　Write a false statement about the lines of symmetry in Shape B.

☐

| Activity | Lewis thinks of a number. It's <u>odd</u>, <u>less than 50</u> and a <u>multiple of 3</u>. List all the numbers Lewis could be thinking of. |

Learning Objective:

"I can make up my own statements about patterns of numbers and shapes using examples."

© 2008 CGP

Number Patterns

1 | Complete the next 4 terms in each sequence:

a) 13 19 25 ⬚ ⬚ ⬚ ⬚ The rule is ⬚

b) 2 0 –2 ⬚ ⬚ ⬚ ⬚ The rule is ⬚

c) 480 240 ⬚ ⬚ ⬚ ⬚ The rule is ⬚

d) 7 10 17 ⬚ ⬚ ⬚ ⬚ The rule is ⬚

2 | Charlie owns a factory that makes squirrel-flavoured chocolate bars.

This formula shows the connection between the number of chocolate bars and the number of boxes:

Number of boxes × 9 = Number of chocolate bars

a)   How many chocolate bars are there in 8 boxes?

b)   If I had 90 chocolate bars, how many boxes would I have?

c)   Charlie starts using larger boxes that hold 15 chocolate bars. Write the new formula:

3 | Look at this sequence of shapes:

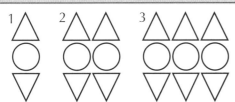

a)   Draw the 4th and 5th terms of the sequence in the box.
b)   How many triangles will be in the 100th term? Explain how you know.

Activity

Look at these 2 statements:

a)   Work out the value of ▩ and ⬤ .

b)   Write your own expressions using numbers and shapes.

Learning Objective:

"I can write a formula using shapes and numbers."

Planning Problem Solving

1 | Put each letter in the correct place on the diagram. The first two have been done for you.

N̶   D̶   A

S   C   G

	Only straight lines	Only curved lines	Straight and curved lines
No lines of symmetry	N		
One or more lines of symmetry			D

2 | The children in Class 4 did a survey about their favourite types of newt. They started to put their results in a frequency table.

Type of newt	Tally	Total
Smooth	‖‖ ‖	7
Palmate	‖‖ ‖‖ ‖	
Crested		
Banded		

a) Complete the total for palmate newts.

b) One more child liked crested newts than liked palmate newts. Complete the tally and total for crested newts.

c) There are 32 children in the class. Complete the banded newt information.

3 | Charlotte needs to buy 10 buns. She has £2.

Cherry — 15p
Iced — 25p
Cream — 20p

a) If she buys 5 cherry buns, can she also buy 5 iced buns?

b) Charlotte buys 4 cream buns, 4 cherry buns and 2 iced buns. How much change will she get from £2?

Activity | In question 1 you sorted some letters. Find some other ways of sorting letters of the alphabet. E.g. letters in your name and letters not in your name. Make a table or diagram to show your sorting.

Learning Objective:

"I can organise information and use it to answer questions."

 © 2008 CGP

Planning Problem Solving

1 | Some children have recorded their ages and heights.

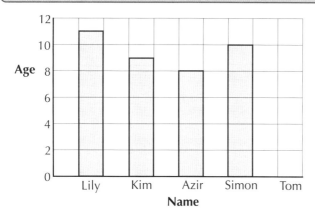
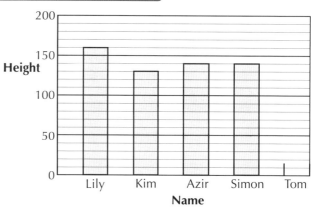

a) Tom is 9 years old and is 150 cm tall. Record this information on the two graphs above.

b) Use the graphs to complete the table on the right.

	Shorter than 150 cm	150 cm or taller
10 or older		Lily
Younger than 10		

2 | This table shows which pets belong to a group of children.

Name	Cat	Dog	Rabbit	Fish	Snake
Charlie		✔			✔
Ella	✔	✔			
Holly			✔		
Archie				✔	
Amy	✔	✔		✔	

a) Which child owns the most pets?

b) Who owns a dog but not a cat?

c) Write down another question that could be answered using this chart, then answer it.

Activity | Here is the menu at the Pudding Parlour:

Vanilla or Strawberry Ice Cream
Chocolate or Toffee Sauce
Marshmallow or Jelly bean toppings

Using an ice cream, a sauce and a topping each time, how many different puddings can you make from these choices?

Learning Objective:

"I can organise and understand information."

Planning Problem Solving

1 | **Look at these digit cards:**

a) Make a 3-digit number greater than 721 but less than 749 using the cards. ☐

b) Write another problem to solve using the cards. Then solve your problem.

2 | **This graph shows the number of boys and girls in each class at a school.**

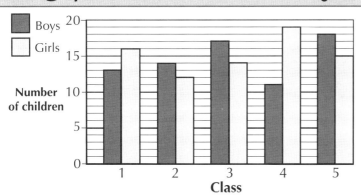

a) Which class contains the fewest children? ☐

b) Which class has 2 more children than Class 3? ☐

c) Write one more question you could ask about this graph. Then answer your question.

3 | **Some children are investigating what fruit and vegetables can be bought for less than £3.**

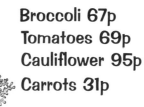

Broccoli 67p
Tomatoes 69p
Cauliflower 95p
Carrots 31p

Bananas 82p
Bag of apples 98p
Pineapple £1.05

a) Tick the true statements:

You can buy a pineapple, a bag of apples and a cauliflower for less than £3. ☐

It costs more to buy bananas and carrots than to buy broccoli and tomatoes. ☐

If you pay for 2 cauliflowers and a bag of apples with £3, you get 17p change. ☐

b) Write down a way that the children could extend their investigation.

Activity | Imagine that you rolled two normal dice and multiplied the numbers rolled.
a) What is the greatest number you could make?
b) Which numbers less than 11 could you make?
c) Write down another question about rolling dice and investigate it.

Learning Objective:

"I can suggest ways to extend investigations."

Problem Solving

You can use a calculator for this sheet

1 | This list shows how far some skiers jumped.

Liz Leap	215.3 m
Sam Snow	87.4 m
Fred Fly	161.5 m
Jane Jump	231.6 m

How much further did Liz Leap jump than Sam Snow?

[ ] m

2 | This chart shows how Year 4 children came to school in May and December.

	May	December
Walk	39	11
Cycle	31	14
Bus	23	51
Car	16	33

a) How many children are there in Year 4?

b) How many more children cycled in May than December?

c) How many children come by either bus or car in May?

3 | Here is the price of a games console and the game "Hamster Attack" in two shops:

Shop A
Games console   £179.99
Hamster Attack   £39.99

Shop B
Games console   £189.95
Hamster Attack   £36.50

How much more would you pay in Shop B for the console and the game together?

Activity   Find out how much a litre of petrol costs.
Ask a car driver how much it costs them to fill up their tank.
Use a calculator to work out how many litres their tank holds.

Learning Objective:

"I can solve problems with one or two steps."

        © 2008 CGP

Problem Solving

You can use a calculator for this sheet

1 | A 1.5 litre bottle of lemonade is poured into 12 glasses. |

How much lemonade goes into each glass?

2 | Bread costs 86p per loaf. |

a) Anne has £6. How many loaves can she buy?

b) How much change will she get?

3 | Mary goes to the supermarket. |

Bananas	42p per kg
Apples	39p per kg
Grapes	87p per kg

a) Mary buys 1.5 kg of each kind of fruit. What is the total cost?

b) Mary buys 2 kg of bananas, 3 kg of grapes and 2 kg of apples.
This is enough to make 10 glasses of a fruit drink.
Calculate the cost of one glass of the fruit drink.

| Activity | Find and measure the mass of some apples.
If they cost <u>29p per kilogram</u>, how much would these apples cost?

Learning Objective:

"I can identify the steps I need to take to solve problems."

© 2008 CGP

Problem Solving

Don't use a calculator for this sheet

1  Alan's garden is 14.6 m long and 3.8 m wide.

Find the perimeter of Alan's garden.

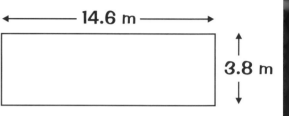
← 14.6 m →
3.8 m

2 Sue buys a book that costs £5.99 and a magazine that costs £2.35.

How much change will she get from £20?

3 Tim makes a glass of squash using 20 ml of juice and 185 ml of water.

a) How many glasses of squash can he make from a 2 litre bottle of juice?

b) How much water would he need?

4 Ten cakes cost £12. How much does one cake cost?

Activity | Find 5 books. Look at their prices.
What is the <u>total cost</u> of the 5 books?

Learning Objective:

"I can identify the steps I need to take to solve problems."

                                                                    © 2008 CGP

Problem Solving

You can use a calculator for this sheet

1 | The prices of clothes in a shop are increased by 20%.

Work out the new price for each item of clothing.

a)
£16.50

b)
£11.20

c)
£1.25

2 | A rectangle is made up of 3 identical squares.

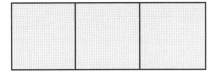

The perimeter of the rectangle is 60 cm.

a) What is the perimeter of one of the squares?

b) What is the area of the rectangle?

3 | James buys 2 fish and gets £14.02 change from £20.

Both fish cost the same price. What was the cost of one fish?

Activity

A birdseed mix is made from 25% sesame seeds, 10% peanuts, 30% maize and 35% oatmeal.

Design a <u>chart</u> to show how much of each ingredient there would be in bags containing 500 g, 1 kg and 5 kg of birdseed.

Learning Objective:

"I can solve problems involving more than one step."

© 2008 CGP

Write and Draw to Solve Problems

1 | **This pattern is made using matchsticks.**

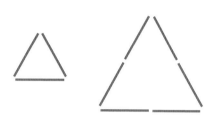

a) Draw the next triangle.

b) How many matchsticks would you use for the fourth triangle?

2 | **The sum of Pete's and Dan's ages is 12. Dan is 5.**

a) How old is Pete? Circle how to work out the answer.

$$12 + 5 \qquad 17 - 5 \qquad 17 - 12 \qquad 12 - 5$$

b) In how many years will Dan be **22**? Circle how to work out the answer.

$$12 + 5 \qquad 22 - 5 \qquad 17 + 5 \qquad 22 + 5$$

3 | **A chocolate bar costs 25p.**

a) How much do 2 chocolate bars cost?   p

b) How much do 3 chocolate bars cost?   p

c) Write a number sentence to work out how much 7 chocolate bars cost.

Activity Use matchsticks or pens and pencils to make this pattern.
How many more of them
do you need each time?

Learning Objective:

"I can solve problems using numbers and diagrams."

© 2008 CGP

Write and Draw to Solve Problems

1 | 220 children go on a school trip. 12 teachers go with them. They go on 53-seater coaches. |

How many coaches will they need? Show your working.

They will need [ ] coaches.

2 | Sam is going to stay at a hotel for 6 nights. |

Breakfast £5   Sid's Café   HOTEL   Bed Only £35 / Bed and Breakfast £45

a) Fill in the table to show the cost of just a bed at the hotel.

Number of nights	1	2	3	4	5	6
Total cost	£35	£70				

b) How much will 6 breakfasts at Sid's Cafe cost?

c) How much money will Sam save by eating breakfast at Sid's Cafe instead of at the Hotel every day?

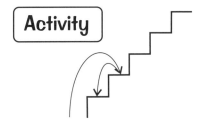

Activity

Some children are playing a game.
They jump up 2 steps and down 1 step.
Draw the rest of the jumps to get up these 5 steps.
How many jumps are needed?
Try it with different numbers of steps.

Learning Objective:

"I can solve problems using numbers and diagrams."

Write and Draw to Solve Problems

1 | Peter buys a CD and a book for £16.90. |

The book costs £3.75.
Circle the number sentence you could use to find the cost of the CD.

$$3.75 + 16.90 = \boxed{} \qquad 16.90 - 3.75 = \boxed{}$$

$$16.90 \div 3.75 = \boxed{} \qquad 3.75 \times \boxed{} = 16.90$$

2 | Vouchers can be bought in 3 amounts: 50p, £1 and £5. |

Mrs Jones counts up the value of her vouchers. She has £38.50.
Find 3 possible combinations of vouchers that make this total.

---

3 | Jim's class are visiting an alien museum. |

Each child has to pay £6.50 for the coach and £2.70 to get into the museum.
30 children are going on the trip.

a) What is the cost of the coach?

b) How much does the trip cost in total?

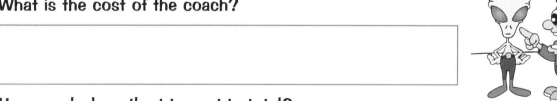

| Activity | Cut a straw into 5 lengths: 2 cm, 3 cm, 4 cm, 5 cm and 6 cm.
Arrange 3 straws at a time to make a triangle.
How many different triangles can you make? Find a way to record
the triangles that you make so that you don't repeat any. |

Learning Objective:

"I can break a problem into steps and say the
calculation I need to do to work out each step."

© 2008 CGP

Write and Draw to Solve Problems

1 | George cycles the same distance each day. |

This distance is represented by ▲ .

Circle the number sentence which represents how far George travels in a week.

▲ + 7   7 × ▲   ▲ ÷ 7   7 − ▲

2 | ⬤ and △ each stand for a different number. |

⬤ = 12.   ⬤ + ⬤ = △ + △ + ⬤

What is the value of △?

3 | Doris can type 45 words in one minute. |

a) Draw a table that Doris could use to find out how many words she can type in 5, 10, 15, 20, 30 and 60 minutes.

b) How could Doris use the table to find out how long it would take her to type out a 1000 word story?

| Activity | Drinks cost 45p and ice creams cost 85p. How much would it cost to buy a drink and an ice cream for each member of your family? |

Learning Objective:

"I can use a table to help me solve a problem."

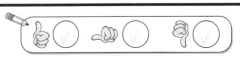

© 2008 CGP

Counting and Sequences

1 | Write the next three numbers in these sequences:

a) 48   52   56   60   [ ] [ ] [ ]

b) 700   725   750   775   [ ] [ ] [ ]

2 | What number is each insect hiding?

a)  111   121   131   141

b) 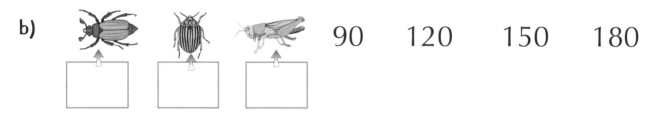 90   120   150   180

3 | Jump along the number line in the steps given.

a) 20
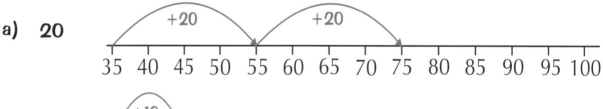

b) 10
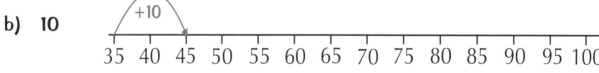

c) 15
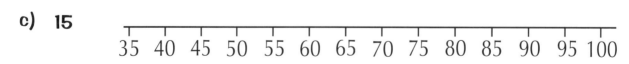

Activity   Start from 0 on a number line and hop along in steps of 2. Do you always land on even numbers or on odd numbers? What about if you jump along in steps of 3?

Learning Objective:

"I can count up or down in steps of different sizes."

Counting and Sequences

1 | **Fill in the missing numbers in these sequences:**

a) [ ] [ ] [ ] −1   1   3   5

b) [ ] [ ] −1   2   5   8   [ ]

c) 9.6   10.2   10.8   11.4   [ ] [ ] [ ]

d) 3.6   3.3   3.0   2.7   [ ] [ ] [ ]

2 | **On Monday the temperature is 15 °C.**

Every day it gets colder by **3 °C**. Fill in the temperatures below.

Day	Monday	Tuesday	Wednesday	Thursday	Friday	Saturday	Sunday
Temperature	**15 °C**						

3 | **Write the first two numbers in this sequence in figures.**

[ ] [ ]   minus two, plus seven, plus sixteen, plus twenty-five

4 | **Stu lifts giant doughnuts.**

Each doughnut has a mass of 0.6 kg. Complete this table.

Number of doughnuts	1	2	3	4	5
Mass	**0.6 kg**				

Activity | An average 10 year old is about 1.4 m tall. Giraffes are about 5.6 m tall. Make a sequence to find out how many times taller a giraffe is than a 10 year old. It will start like this: 5.6, 4.2, ... Find out the heights of some buildings and do the same thing.

Learning Objective:

"I can find missing numbers in sequences that include negative and decimal numbers."

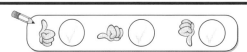

Counting and Sequences

1 | **Fill in the missing numbers in these sequences:**

a) ☐ ☐ ☐ −11 −2 7 16

b) 20.0 21.4 22.8 24.2 ☐ ☐ ☐

c) −1.1 −0.8 −0.5 −0.2 ☐ ☐ ☐

d) ☐ ☐ ☐ −1.2 0.7 2.6 4.5

2 | **Sue saves £4.25 a week.**

a) Write a sequence to show how her savings increase each week for 6 weeks.

☐

  b) Sue wants to buy a computer game costing £18.50. How many weeks must she save for? ☐

3 | **Write down the rule for each sequence.**

a) −20 −16 −12 ☐

b) 12.3 12.1 11.9 ☐

Activity Count back from 20 in steps of 0.9. Write down the sequence.
What pattern can you see in the digits?
Try counting down in steps of different sizes.

Learning Objective:

"I can find missing numbers in sequences that include negative and decimal numbers."

© 2008 CGP

Name: .... Date: **23**

Decimals

1 Jess has a ribbon measuring 2.4 m. She cuts it into 10 cm strips.

How many strips will Jess be able to cut from the ribbon?

2 Put these amounts of money in order. Start with the smallest.

£1.21   21p   £1.02   120p   £1.22

Smallest ⟶ Largest

3 Draw a line from each decimal to its place on the number line.

0.45   0.49   0.55

0.4 ——————————————— 0.6

0.42   0.54   0.59

4 Fill in the boxes to show the decimals on the number line.

0.1   0.15   0.2   0.25   0.3

Activity Find a receipt from the supermarket.
Choose any 10 items and put them in order of cost.

Learning Objective:

"I can use decimals when I work with money and measurement."

SHEET **2**   © 2008 CGP

Decimals

Key Objective

1 | **Six frogs measured how far they could jump.**

Debbie	1.85 m
Rob	1.96 m
Gill	2.23 m
Pete	2.05 m
Julia	2.19 m
David	2.16 m

a)   Put them in order. Start with the furthest jump.

b)   Who jumped closest to 2 metres?

2 | **2.63 partitions into 2 + 0.6 + 0.03.**

Partition the following decimals.

a)   6.82

b)   9.16

3 | **In the number 35.2 the value of the 3 is 3 tens.**

What is the value of the underlined digit in each of the numbers?

a)   <u>3</u>20      b)   <u>2</u>561      c)   1<u>4</u>.9

d)   73.<u>8</u>      e)   59.2<u>5</u>      f)   <u>3</u>8.16

Activity   Find a shopping receipt. Choose 3 items from the list and partition their prices. £2.99 would partition to 2 + 0.9 + 0.09.

Learning Objective:

"I can say the value of each digit in a number, including decimals."

© 2008 CGP

Decimals

1 Fill in the boxes to show the decimals on the number line.

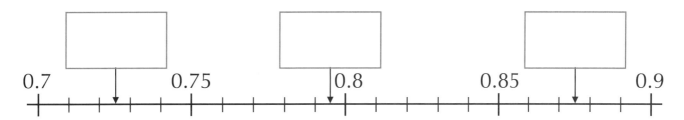

0.7   0.75   0.8   0.85   0.9

2 Circle the smallest decimal in each set.

a)   2.365   1.412   2.635

b)   13.261   13.621   13.126

c)   0.656   0.565   0.556

4₂8

3 In the number 2.0**5**, the value of the underlined digit is 5 hundredths.

What are the values of these underlined digits?

a) **4**.96

b) **1**2.30

c) 6.**9**95

d) 18.4**0**2

e) 27.99**8**

f) **6**47.4

4 Write numbers in the boxes to make the sums correct.

a) **0.539 = 0.5 + 0.03 +**

b) **1.87 = 1.0 + 0.8 +**

Activity Use some scales to <u>measure your mass</u> in kg to 2 decimal places.
Now partition your mass (like Q4 above).

Learning Objective:

"I can put numbers with up to 3 decimal places
onto a number line and I can partition them."

© 2008 CGP

Fractions

1 Circle all the shapes that are three quarters shaded.

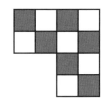

2 Draw an arrow from each mixed number to its place on the number line.

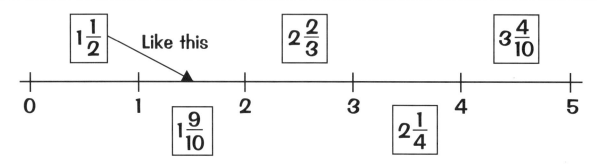

3 Put the mixed numbers in order. Start with the smallest.

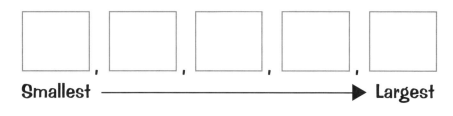

Smallest ⟶ Largest

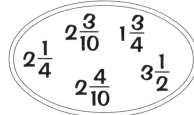

4 Draw lines to join the fractions to the right shapes.

$\frac{4}{12}$ shaded $\frac{3}{8}$ shaded $\frac{7}{10}$ shaded

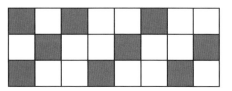   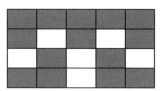   

Activity   Draw a circle and colour three quarters.
Repeat this with a quarter, a third and a half.

Learning Objective:

"I can put mixed numbers like $1\frac{3}{4}$ on a number line."

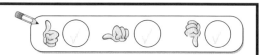

                    © 2008 CGP

Fractions

1 | A birthday cake is cut into 8 pieces. Five pieces are eaten. |

   a) What fraction of the cake has been eaten?

   b) What fraction of the cake is left?

2 | Draw lines to match equivalent fractions. | One pair has been done for you.

$$\frac{3}{4} \qquad \frac{2}{3} \qquad \frac{4}{5} \qquad \frac{5}{8}$$

$$\frac{10}{16} \qquad \frac{9}{12} \qquad \frac{4}{6} \qquad \frac{8}{10}$$

3 | Draw rings around the two equivalent fractions. |

$$\frac{5}{6} \qquad \frac{2}{3} \qquad \frac{1}{4} \qquad \frac{10}{15} \qquad \frac{3}{4}$$

4 | Fill in the gaps to complete the equivalent fractions. |

  a) $\frac{3}{4} = \frac{\square}{8}$ b) $\frac{3}{5} = \frac{15}{\square}$

  c) $\frac{\square}{25} = \frac{80}{100}$ d) $\frac{9}{\square} = \frac{27}{30}$

| Activity | Here are some equivalent fractions: $\frac{1}{5}, \frac{2}{10}, \frac{3}{15}$.
How many more can you find in 5 minutes?

Learning Objective:

"I can find fractions that are equivalent to each other."

© 2008 CGP

Fractions

1  **Reduce these fractions to their simplest form.**

a) $\dfrac{9}{12}$ ☐

b) $\dfrac{10}{20}$ ☐

c) $\dfrac{24}{36}$ ☐

d) $\dfrac{21}{49}$ ☐

e) $\dfrac{32}{80}$ ☐

2 **Look at the fractions in the circle.**

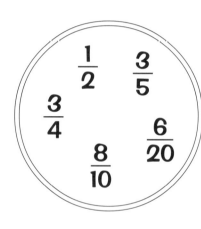

$\dfrac{1}{2}$ $\dfrac{3}{5}$

$\dfrac{3}{4}$ $\dfrac{6}{20}$

$\dfrac{8}{10}$

a) Rewrite the fractions so they have the same denominator.

☐ ☐ ☐ ☐ ☐

b) Then put them in order, starting with the smallest.

☐ , ☐ , ☐ , ☐ , ☐

Smallest ⸻⸻⸻⸻⟶ Largest

3 **Some cakes are sliced into 5 pieces.**

a) Pete eats 6 slices.
How many cakes has Pete eaten?
Give your answer as a fraction.

☐

b) Paul eats 14 slices.
How many cakes has Paul eaten?
Give your answer as a fraction.

☐

Activity   Find 10 different fractions that can be simplified to a third.

Learning Objective:

"I can simplify fractions and put them in order of size."

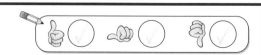

     © 2008 CGP

Fractions and Decimals

1 | For each decimal write an equivalent fraction. |

a) 0.04

b) 0.75

c) 0.6

d) 0.25

2 | Use a line to join each fraction to its equivalent decimal. |

$\dfrac{2}{10}$ $\dfrac{3}{4}$ $\dfrac{10}{100}$ $\dfrac{5}{100}$

0.75 0.1 0.2 0.05

3 | Look at the calculator displays below. |

Write the equivalent fraction to the decimal shown on each screen.

a) 0.25

b) 0.02

4 | Write each fraction as a decimal. |

a) six tenths

b) four hundredths

c) three quarters

d) twelve hundredths

| Activity | 0.001 is equivalent to $\dfrac{1}{1000}$. 0.002 is equivalent to $\dfrac{2}{1000}$.

Can you spot the rule for this?
Give the fractions that 0.009 and 0.023 are equivalent to.
Check your answers on a calculator.

Learning Objective:

"I can recognise decimals and fractions that are equivalent."

© 2008 CGP

Fractions and Decimals

1 Complete the two grids so that the fractions on the left are equivalent to the decimals on the right.

$\frac{1}{2}$		$\frac{6}{10}$
	$\frac{2}{10}$	
$\frac{5}{20}$		$\frac{15}{100}$
	$\frac{3}{4}$	

	0.95	
0.7		0.25
	0.35	
0.8		0.4

There ain't enough room for the both of us in this town.

0.3 $\frac{3}{10}$

2 Shade the correct amount of each shape.

a) 0.75

b) 0.6

c) 0.25

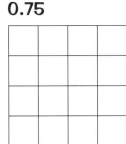 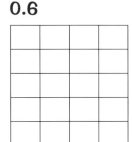 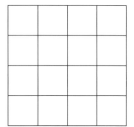

3 Write a decimal to describe how much of each shape has been shaded.

a)

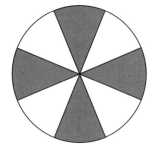

b)

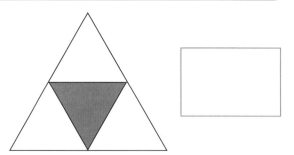

Activity Practise using your calculator to convert fractions to decimals. Try these ones, and then make up some fractions of your own.

a) $\frac{23}{100}$ b) $\frac{4}{13}$ c) $\frac{71}{90}$ d) $\frac{339}{1100}$

Learning Objective:

"I can give the decimal equivalent of a simple fraction."

© 2008 CGP

Fractions and Decimals

1 **Look at the fractions below.**

a) Change the fractions into their decimal equivalent.

$$\frac{12}{20}$$ $$\frac{9}{10}$$ $$\frac{3}{4}$$ $$\frac{2}{5}$$ $$\frac{70}{100}$$

b) Put the decimals in order. Start with the smallest.

2 **Change the fractions to their decimal equivalents. Then write them in the correct places on the number line.**

$$\frac{15}{20}$$ ☐ $$\frac{20}{100}$$ ☐ $$\frac{22}{40}$$ ☐ $$\frac{4}{10}$$ ☐ $$\frac{9}{30}$$ ☐

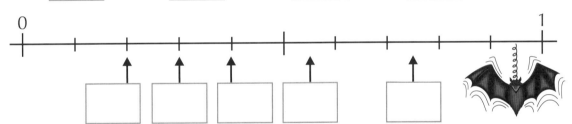

0   1

3 **Use your calculator to convert these fractions to decimals.**

Circle the largest fraction in each set.

a)

$$\frac{2}{3} = \boxed{} \qquad \frac{5}{8} = \boxed{}$$

$$\frac{6}{11} = \boxed{} \qquad \frac{8}{13} = \boxed{}$$

b)

$$\frac{3}{7} = \boxed{} \qquad \frac{11}{15} = \boxed{}$$

$$\frac{9}{16} = \boxed{} \qquad \frac{4}{21} = \boxed{}$$

Activity

Choose a 2 digit number and use the digits as decimal places.

E.g. 32 becomes 0.32. Change the decimal into a fraction.

So 0.32 becomes $\frac{32}{100}$ which can be simplified to $\frac{16}{50}$ and $\frac{8}{25}$.

Do the same for 5 other decimals.

Learning Objective:

"I can convert fractions into decimals."

© 2008 CGP

Numbers and Number Lines

1 Write these numbers in order, smallest first:

−4   6   −2   2   10   0

smallest □ → □ → □ → □ → □ → □ biggest

2 Fill in the labels on this number line:

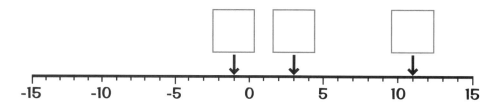

-15   -10   -5   0   5   10   15

3 Put the correct sign (> or <) in the boxes. Use the number line to help.

-15   -10   -5   0   5   10   15

a) −3 □ 2   b) −1 □ −4   c) 0 □ 10   d) 0 □ −10

4 Write the correct numbers in the boxes below this thermometer.

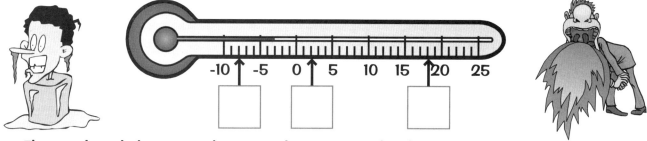

-10 ↑ -5   0 ↑ 5   10   15 ↑ 20   25

The numbers below go in the empty boxes. Use the thermometer to help fill them in.

−1   −10

a) □ < −5   b) 0 > □

Activity The temperature of a freezer is shown on the number line (−18).
Mark on a fridge (4) and an oven (200).
Mark two other temperatures on this line.

freezer

-20 -10 0 10 20 30 40 50 60 70 80 90 100 110 120 130 140 150 160 170 180 190 200

Learning Objective:

"I can put positive and negative numbers into order.
I can use the < and > signs."

SHEET **3**   © 2008 CGP

Numbers and Number Lines

1 | Put these numbers in order, smallest first.

5.6   6.1   6.3   5.4   5.2

smallest [ ] ➝ [ ] ➝ [ ] ➝ [ ] ➝ [ ] biggest

2 | Fill in the missing numbers in these sequences:

a)   7.2   7.5   7.8   [ ]   8.4   [ ]   [ ]

b)   [ ]   27.4   27.0   [ ]   26.2   25.8   25.4

c)   4   −1   −6   [ ]   [ ]   −21   −26

d)   1.2   0.7   0.2   [ ]   [ ]   −1.3   −1.8

3 | Write the missing numbers in these boxes:

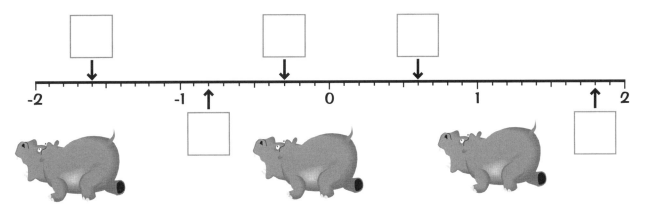

[ ]   [ ]   [ ]

-2   -1 ↑   0   1   ↑ 2
            [ ]   [ ]

Activity Make up some <u>number sequences</u> and show them on <u>number lines</u>.
Like this:

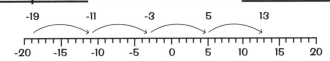

-19   -11   -3   5   13

-20 -15 -10 -5   0   5   10 15 20

Learning Objective:

"I can count up or down in decimal steps with positive
and negative numbers."

     © 2008 CGP

Numbers and Number Lines

1   **The Duke of Ellingham's castle has 5 upper floors, a ground floor called floor 0, a kitchen called floor –1 and a dungeon called floor –2.**

a)   Rapunzel leaves her room on floor 5 and goes down 6 floors. What floor has she gone to?

b)   Baldrick works in the dungeon on floor –2.
He needs to see the duke on floor 3.
How many floors does he need to go up?

2   **The milk in Michael's freezer is at –18 degrees Celsius. The milk in his fridge is at 4 degrees Celsius.**

a)   What is the difference between the two temperatures?

b)   He takes the milk out of the freezer and overnight it has warmed up by twenty degrees.
What temperature is the milk now?

3   **Planet Chillon has a surface temperature of 3 degrees Celsius. The nearby planet Freezon is 5 degrees colder.**

a)   What is the temperature on Planet Freezon?

Ice to see you.

b)   The robots from Planet Bogbot shoot both planets with a freezing ray.
Planet Chillon's temperature is now –15 degrees Celsius,
Planet Freezon's temperature is now –17 degrees Celsius.
Which planet has had the greater temperature decrease?

Activity   Design a castle with some floors above ground and some floors below ground. Make up some questions about your castle (like those in Q1).

Learning Objective:

"I can find the difference between positive and negative integers."

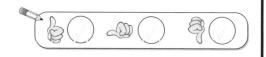

    © 2008 CGP

Percentages

1 | Some children take a spelling test. Here are their results:

Name	Percentage of correct spellings	Percentage of incorrect spellings
Simon	65%	
Helen		20%
Penny	50%	
Tim		15%

a) Fill in the missing percentages.

b) The spelling test is out of 30. How many words did Penny spell correctly?

2 | Look at this diagram:

a) Shade **25%** of the diagram.

b) How many more squares would you have to shade to cover 50% of the shape?

3 | Convert the following into percentages:

a) $0.25 =$ [   ] %

b) $\dfrac{99}{100} =$ [   ] %

c) $\dfrac{56}{100} =$ [   ] %

d) $\dfrac{8}{10} =$ [   ] %

e) $\dfrac{4}{10} =$ [   ] %

f) $0.42 =$ [   ] %

4 | Is $\dfrac{1}{4}$ smaller than 19%? Give your reason.

Activity Look at the <u>labels</u> in some of your clothes. Find the <u>percentages</u> of the materials they are made from and check they add up to 100%.

Learning Objective:

"I can convert fractions and decimals into percentages."

© 2008 CGP

36   Name: ....   Date: ....

Percentages

1 | Rita worked out the percentages of animals in her local pet shops. |

Fill in the remaining percentages for each shop in the correct box.

Cat Castle   Mousetastic

   Pet Palace   Dave's Dog Shop

52% cats   70% mice   21% hamsters   63% dogs
19% dogs   2% rats   3% dogs   12% dragons

[   ] % other   [   ] % other   [   ] % other   [   ] % other

2 | Shade in 10% of each shape: |

a) [grid]   b) [grid]

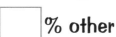

3 | Grant is running the egg and spoon race at his school sports day. |

The race is 50m long. Grant manages to run 20m before he drops his egg.
What percentage of the race did he complete?   [   ] %

4 | Convert the following into percentages: |

a) $\frac{27}{100}$ = [   ] %   c) 0.3 = [   ] %

b) $\frac{9}{10}$ = [   ] %   d) 0.75 = [   ] %

| Activity | Write down as many <u>fractions</u> which are equivalent to 50% as you
can in 1 minute. Do the same for those which equal 25%.

Learning Objective:

"I can convert fractions and decimals to percentages."

SHEET 2   © 2008 CGP

Key Objective

<u>Percentages</u>

A calculator might help with some of these questions

1 Convert these percentages into decimals:

a) $12\% = $ ☐

b) $35\% = $ ☐

c) $78\% = $ ☐

d) $4\% = $ ☐

2 Circle the fractions that are worth 25% or more:

$\dfrac{4}{10}$ $\dfrac{3}{5}$ $\dfrac{2}{3}$ $\dfrac{4}{7}$ $\dfrac{4}{11}$

$\dfrac{2}{12}$ $\dfrac{1}{6}$ $\dfrac{2}{8}$ $\dfrac{2}{9}$

3 Work out the answers to the following problems:

a) Alice spends £2.50 of her £10 pocket money.
   What percentage has she spent? ☐ %

b) 27g of a 270g chocolate bar has melted in the sun.
   What percentage has melted? ☐ %

c) Lisa has 20 cows. 11 of them run away.
   What percentage has she lost? ☐ %

d) Rob's penny jar can store 500 pennies.
   He has saved 300 pennies.
   What percentage has he saved so far? ☐ %

Activity Write down different amounts of money in which the first amount is worth <u>10%</u> of the second.

<u>Learning Objective:</u>

"I can express one quantity as a percentage of another."

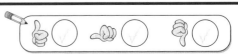

© 2008 CGP

Proportion and Ratio

1 | Here are two hotels: |

light on

light off

Seafront Hotel   Jo's Motel

a) What fraction of lights are off at the Seafront Hotel?

b) Shade the windows of Jo's Motel so that 3 in every 4 lights are off.

2 | Solve the following problems. Show your working for each. |

a) An ice lolly costs 56p. How much would 3 ice lollies cost?

b) A bucket holds 100 shells when it's full. Martha has 27 shells.
Estimate what fraction of the bucket Martha can fill.

3 | In a harbour there are 2 yachts for every 3 fishing boats. |

How many fishing boats are in the harbour if there are:

a) 6 yachts?

b) 10 yachts?

| Activity | Ask 5 people if they like banana milkshakes. Write down how
many said yes to how many said no. Use this to estimate
how many of 20 people would like banana milkshakes.
Try it for different numbers of people.

Learning Objective:

"I can estimate proportions and fractions."

Name: .... Date: **39**

Proportion and Ratio

1 | Ruby's scarf has 15 stripes. |

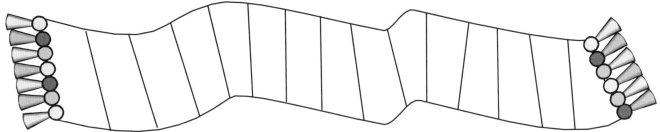

a) Colour in the scarf so there are **2** blue stripes for every **3** yellow stripes.

b) Fill in the boxes to complete these rules:

2 in every **5** stripes are coloured [   ]

[   ] in every **5** stripes are coloured yellow.

2 | At a football match there are **3** away fans for every **5** home fans. |

a) Complete the table.

b) If there are **80** fans in total, how many away fans are there?

[   ]

Away	Home	Total
3	5	
	10	
12		
		40

3 | Here is a list of ingredients for curry sauce: |

Recipe for curry sauce
Serves 6 people
150g tomatoes
600ml water
3 small onions
12g curry powder

Ethan wants to make curry sauce for **12** people.

a) How many grams of tomatoes will he need?

[   ]

b) How many millilitres of water will he need?

[   ]

| Activity | A chef needs 1 onion for every 4 hotdogs. Make a <u>table</u> showing how many onions he needs for 4, 8, 12, 16 or 20 hotdogs.

Learning Objective:

"I can express ratios in numbers and words."

SHEET **3**

© 2008 CGP

Proportion and Ratio

1   **Solve the following problems. Show your working for each.**

    a)   7 postcards cost £2.80. How much does 1 postcard cost?

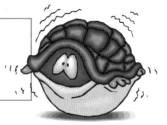

    b)   Alligators cost £120 for 10. What is the cost of 25 alligators?

2   **A fruit salad is made up of $\frac{1}{4}$ strawberries, $\frac{1}{4}$ bananas and $\frac{1}{2}$ oranges.**

    Nicola uses 150g of oranges. How many strawberries will she need? Give your reason.

3   **Here is part of a number line. Fill in the missing numbers in the boxes.**

    a)   b)   c)

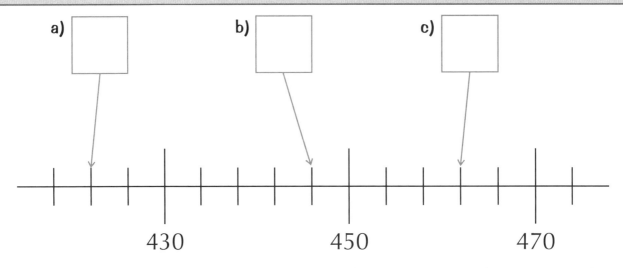

          430   450   470

Activity   Count how many boys and girls there are in your favourite TV show. Work out the fraction of characters who are boys and the fraction who are girls. Do the same for people in your favourite film and in your class.

Learning Objective:

"I can work out proportions and use these to solve problems."

Rounding

1 | **Round these numbers to the nearest 1000.**

a) 2370 [ ] b) 3614 [ ]

c) 5732 [ ] d) 6197 [ ]

2 | **Round these numbers to the nearest 100.**

a) 5714 [ ] b) 2657 [ ]

c) 5794 [ ] d) 6779 [ ]

3 | **Round each number to the nearest 10 by matching it to a number in a box below.**

5327   5372   5355   5318

| 5320 | 5330 | 5340 | 5350 | 5360 | 5370 |

4 | **Round the height of each mountain to the nearest 1000 m and to the nearest 100 m.**

Mountain	Height	Nearest 1000 m	Nearest 100 m
K2	8611 m		
Annapurna I	8091 m		
Snowdon	1085 m		
Mont Blanc	4810 m		

Activity 2950 rounds to **3000** to the nearest 1000.
Find 5 other numbers which round to **3000** to the nearest 1000.
Find 5 numbers which round to **3000** to the nearest 10.

Learning Objective:

"I can round a 4-digit number to the nearest 10, 100 or 1000."

© 2008 CGP

Key Objective

<u>Rounding</u>

1 | Round these numbers to the nearest 100.

a) 267 ▢   b) 8542 ▢   c) 3881 ▢

2 | Round each number to 1 decimal place and then to the nearest whole number.

Number	to 1 decimal place	to the nearest whole number
14.71		
7.29		
21.98		

3 | Round the cost of each surfboard to the nearest pound and then to the nearest 10p.

surfboard	to the nearest pound	to the nearest 10p
£23.99		
£31.50		
£50.25		

Activity

Look in the food cupboard and find a tin or packet which shows nutritional information. Round each mass to the nearest gram.

For example:

Protein   4.3 g ➡ 4 g

Fat   0.5 g ➡ 1 g

<u>Learning Objective:</u>

"I can round numbers with up to 2 decimal places."

© 2008 CGP

Rounding

1 | Round these numbers to the nearest tenth and to the nearest whole number.

number	to the nearest tenth		number	to the nearest whole number

a) 5.24 ➡ [ ]

b) 5.24 ➡ [ ]

c) 7.85 ➡ [ ]

d) 7.85 ➡ [ ]

e) 9.53 ➡ [ ]

f) 9.53 ➡ [ ]

2 | Round the numbers on the left to two decimal places.

Match them to the numbers on the right.

2 decimal places

3.672	3.76
3.267	3.28
3.762	3.27
3.726	3.67
3.276	3.73

3 | Here are the prices of some ice cream cones:

Sam wants to buy one vanilla, two strawberry and two mint cones.

Vanilla 85p
Strawberry 95p
Mint £1.20

a) Round each price to the nearest pound and find the approximate total cost.

b) Sam says that this means that £5 will be enough. Is he correct? If he isn't correct, how much more does he need?

Activity | Find the prices of four items in a shop or catalogue. Estimate the total cost by rounding each price and adding them. Now add up the actual amounts. How different is the estimate from the actual cost?

Learning Objective:

"I can round numbers with up to 3 decimal places."

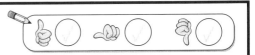

© 2008 CGP

Adding and Subtracting

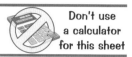

Don't use a calculator for this sheet

1 **Write in the missing numbers:**

a) 5000 is 1000 more than ☐

b) 3000 is 200 more than ☐

c) 700 is 90 less than ☐

2 **Find the change from £10.00 if I buy:**

a) A book for £4.50

b) A bus ticket for 90p.

c) A DVD for £8.40.

£ ☐   £ ☐   £ ☐

3 **Fill in the boxes:**

a) $240 + 90 =$ ☐

b) $2070 + 3020 =$ ☐

c) $1010 - 80 =$ ☐

d) $540 - 330 =$ ☐

4 **Join pairs of numbers with a difference of 80.**

110	940
250	560
640	1030
950	170
1020	30

Activity Look at the map.
Find the lengths of different routes.
E.g. House to shop, via church
= 200 m + 410 m = 610 m
Then make up your own map and do the same.

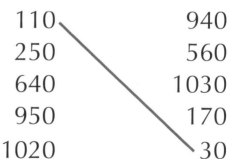

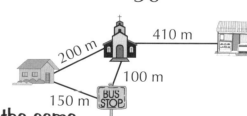

410 m
200 m
100 m
150 m

BUS STOP

Learning Objective:

"I can add and subtract multiples of 10, 100 and 1000."

© 2008 CGP

Adding and Subtracting

Don't use a calculator for this sheet

Key Objective

1 Fill in the boxes:

a) $2.2 + 1.7 = \boxed{}$

b) $7.4 + 1.3 = \boxed{}$

c) $5.1 - 4.9 = \boxed{}$

d) $8.4 - 7.7 = \boxed{}$

2 The slug race track is 10 cm long.

How much further must each slug go?

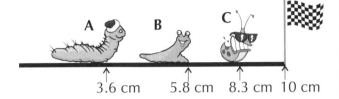

A   B   C

3.6 cm   5.8 cm   8.3 cm 10 cm

A = $\boxed{}$ cm   B = $\boxed{}$ cm   C = $\boxed{}$ cm

3 Make all these additions and subtractions equal 7.

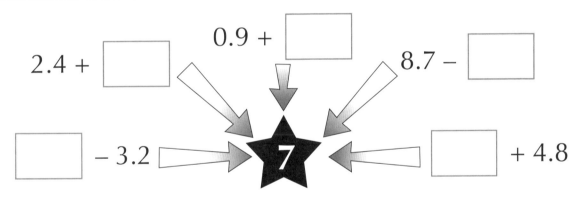

$0.9 + \boxed{}$

$2.4 + \boxed{}$

$8.7 - \boxed{}$

$\boxed{} - 3.2$

7

$\boxed{} + 4.8$

4 Circle the two numbers which add together to make 27.

11.9   12.7   13.5   14.3   14.1

5 Circle the two numbers with a difference of 3.6.

5.2   6.3   7.5   8.7   9.9

Activity Pick a number between 1 and 10.
Write down 5 decimal sums that equal this number.
Can you write down your sums in a pattern to do this more quickly?

Learning Objective:

"I can add and subtract decimals in my head by using a related two-digit addition or subtraction."

© 2008 CGP

Adding and Subtracting

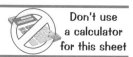

Don't use a calculator for this sheet

Key Objective

1 | Fill in the boxes: |

a) $4.3 + 2.5 =$ ⬜ b) $3.6 + 1.8 =$ ⬜

c) $7.2 - 5.7 =$ ⬜ d) $4.8 - 2.9 =$ ⬜

2 | The amounts on some receipts got smudged. |

Fill in the correct amounts.

a)

book	£4.90
ice-cream	£0.90
TOTAL	▇

b)

newspaper	£1.70
sweets	£1.20
milk	£0.70
TOTAL	▇

c)

shoes	£23.10
socks	▇
TOTAL	£28.20

d)

grapes	£2.70
pears	▇
TOTAL	£5.20

3 | A fly is walking along the wire shown in the diagram. |

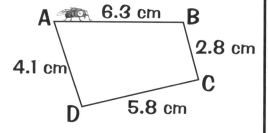

a) How far is it from A to B to C along the wire?

⬜ cm

b) How far is it from A to D to C along the wire?

⬜ cm

c) What is the difference in length between these two routes?

⬜ cm

| Activity | Imagine you are a fly walking around the edge of this sheet of paper. How far must you walk to get all the way round? |

Learning Objective:

"I can add and subtract decimals in my head by using a related two-digit addition or subtraction."

© 2008 CGP

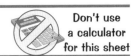
Don't use
a calculator
for this sheet

Key
Objective

Adding and Subtracting

1 **Fill in the boxes:**

a) $5.4 + 2.8 = $ ▢

b) $9.4 - 3.7 = $ ▢

c) $8.2 - $ ▢ $ = 3.9$

d) $6.6 - $ ▢ $ = 5.8$

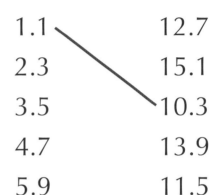

2 **Join pairs of numbers which:**

a) add together to make **9.2**

1.1	6.9
2.3	4.5
3.5	5.7
4.7	3.3
5.9	8.1

(1.1 joined to 8.1)

b) have a difference of **9.2**

1.1	12.7
2.3	15.1
3.5	10.3
4.7	13.9
5.9	11.5

(1.1 joined to 10.3)

3 **Answer these questions:**

a) What is eight point six minus four point three? ▢

b) What is four point seven more than four point seven? ▢

4 **Which of the orders below has a total closest to £10?**

£4.99   £6.99   £3.50   £4.75

Show your working.
Prawns + cake **OR** spaghetti + sandwich?

▢

Activity   Pick three items with decimal prices from a catalogue. Write down the prices and add them up. Check you're right by using a calculator.

Learning Objective:

"I can add and subtract decimals in my head by using a related two-digit addition or subtraction."

© 2008 CGP

Checking Calculations

Don't use a calculator for this sheet

1 | Do the two step calculation and then check your answer.

E.g. $3 \xrightarrow{\times 2} \boxed{6} \xrightarrow{+3} \boxed{9}$ $\boxed{9} \xrightarrow{-3} \boxed{6} \xrightarrow{\div 2} 3$

$10 \xrightarrow{-5} \boxed{} \xrightarrow{\times 2} \boxed{}$ $\boxed{} \xrightarrow{\div 2} \boxed{} \xrightarrow{+5} 10$

2 | Paul and Amy went to a car boot sale.

Estimate how much they each spent
and circle the correct amount.

Paul

£3   £1.99   95p

£3.94

£5.94

£7.94

£8.94

Amy

£2.95   £9.98   95p

£10.88

£11.88

£13.88

£16.88

3 | Jim says that four 52-seater coaches are needed to take 210 children to the zoo.

a)   Round the numbers and do a calculation to check this is about right.

b)   Work out the actual number of seats
on 4 coaches to see if Jim is right.

Activity   Find a receipt from a shopping trip.
Use estimation to check that the total looks about right.

Learning Objective:

"I can use reverse calculations and rounding to help me
check calculations."

Checking Calculations

Don't use a calculator for this sheet

1 | Jenny has worked out that 13 + 14 = 27. |

Using only those numbers, and the symbols for adding (+) and subtracting (−), write two other calculations that can be made from this number sentence.

a)

b)

2 | Using rounding, estimate an answer to these divisions and circle the sensible estimate: |

a)	$119 \div 61 =$	20	2	15	4
b)	$265 \div 28 =$	9	11	6	14
c)	$842 \div 19 =$	34	38	42	50
d)	$92 \div 6 =$	12	15	18	20

3 | Emma has worked out that 265 + 318 = 583. Circle the calculation you might use to check her answer. |

318×265 $583 - 318$ $583 \div 265$

4 | Fill in the empty boxes below. |

If I know that **32 ÷ 4 = 8**, then I also know that:

a) 8 ☐ 4 = 32   b) 32 = 4 ☐ 8   c) 32 ☐ 8 = 4

5 | Round these numbers to the nearest hundred to work out roughly what the answer is. Show your working in the box: |

$1687 - 926 =$

| Activity | How far do you and your friends have to travel to get to school? Can you <u>estimate</u> the total distance? |

Learning Objective:

"I can use inverse operations and rounding to help me check calculations."

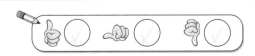

SHEET **5**

© 2008 CGP

Checking Calculations

Don't use a calculator unless the question tells you to

1 | **Tom has worked out that 352 ÷ 8 = 44.** |

Round the figures in Tom's calculation to check that his answer looks about right.

Write an inverse calculation you could do to check Tom's answer.

2 | **The table shows the number of school dinners the cook made each day.** |

a) Complete the rounded number column.

Day of week	Number of dinners	Rounded to the nearest 10
Monday	367	
Tuesday	219	
Wednesday	402	400
Thursday	384	
Friday	421	

b) Use your rounded numbers to estimate the total number of dinners cooked on Monday and Tuesday.

c) Use your calculator to find the exact total number of dinners cooked on Monday and Tuesday.

d) Write an inverse calculation you could use to check this answer is correct.

Activity   Add the number of windows in your home to the number of chairs. Write an <u>inverse calculation</u> to <u>check</u> the total.

Learning Objective:

"I can use inverse operations and rounding to help me check calculations."

SHEET **6**   © 2008 CGP

Checking Calculations

Don't use a calculator for this sheet

1 Find the missing numbers by doing an inverse calculation:

a)
```
  ____
- 725
 231
```

```
  ____
- 15
 67
```

b)
```
 974
-____
 256
```

d)
```
 436
-____
 191
```

2 Amy says that 798 ÷ 41 is about 20.

a) Use rounding to check if she's right.

b) Will the actual answer be more or less than 20? Why?

James thinks that 45 × 29 is about 1350.

c) Use rounding to check if he's right.

3 Kevin added 357 to another 3-digit odd number. His answer was 481.

Has he made a mistake? How do you know?

Activity Write a list of large numbers that are <u>divisible by 2</u>. Do they have anything in <u>common</u>? Try this with some other numbers to see if you can find a <u>pattern</u>.

Learning Objective:

"I can estimate and check the results of calculations."

 © 2008 CGP

Checking Calculations

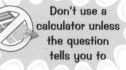

Don't use a calculator unless the question tells you to

1 Sally sold some CDs for £36.60, and then bought some books for £13.80. She thinks she will have £22.80 left.

a) Round the numbers and write a calculation to estimate the amount she will have left.

b) Using the exact figures, do an inverse calculation to check that she is correct.

Sally wants to use the money she has left to buy 21 chocolate bars that cost £1.11 each.

c) Use rounding to estimate how much this costs. Can she afford them based on this estimate?

d) Use a calculator to work out the cost exactly. Can she actually afford them?

2 Use the rules of divisibility to explain how you know the facts below.

The first one's been done for you.

a) 248 is divisible by 2

> The last digit is 8 — which is even.
> Numbers divisible by 2 have an even last digit.

b) 2306 isn't divisible by 9

c) 940 is a multiple of 4

d) 655 is a multiple of 5

Activity Estimate how many minutes you'll sleep in a week. Then estimate how many minutes you'll sleep in a year.

Learning Objective:

"I can estimate and check the results of calculations."

© 2008 CGP

Doubling and Halving

1 Fill in the empty boxes below.

Don't use a calculator for this sheet

a) double 26 ⟶ ☐

b) double 110 ⟶ ☐

c) double ☐ ⟶ 62

d) double ☐ ⟶ 360

2 Here are the full prices of some shopping items. Some are on special offer.

 Tuna 190p

 Bread 150p

Half price Pears usually 18p

Half price Bananas usually 26p

Write how much it costs for Anne to buy these items, and show your working:

a) 2 tins of tuna.

b) 2 loaves of bread.

c) 10 pears.

d) 10 bananas.

3 Ben has a jar with 240 sweets in.
He buys another jar that's exactly the same.

a) How many sweets does he have?

b) Ben gives half a jar of sweets to his sister.
How many sweets does she have?

Activity How many children are in your class? Try <u>doubling</u> and <u>halving</u> this number. Then try the same with some <u>bigger</u> numbers.

Learning Objective:

"I can double and halve two and some three digit numbers."

SHEET 3

© 2008 CGP

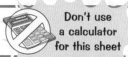

Don't use a calculator for this sheet

Key Objective

<u>*Doubling and Halving*</u>

1 Use the decimals below to make the calculations correct.

7.2   8.4   8.2   7.8   0.6   7.6

a) 3.8 + 3.8 = ☐   **b)** 3.6 + 3.6 = ☐

c) ☐ − 4.2 = 4.2   **d)** ☐ − 4.1 = 4.1

e) 0.6 + ☐ = 1.2   **f)** 15.6 − ☐ = 7.8

2 What is half of 74?

a) ☐   **b)** What is half of 7.4? ☐

3 What is double 24?

a) ☐   **b)** What is double 2.4? ☐

4 What is half of these numbers?

a) 6.8 ☐   **b)** 8.2 ☐   **c)** 0.2 ☐   **d)** 14.4 ☐

5 What is double these numbers?

a) 3.8 ☐   **b)** 4.8 ☐   **c)** 9.7 ☐   **d)** 0.5 ☐

Activity Add up all the spare change you can find at home in pounds and pence. How much would there be if you <u>double</u> or <u>halve</u> it?

<u>*Learning Objective:*</u>

"I can double and halve using decimals."

© 2008 CGP

Key Objective

Doubling and Halving

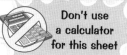
Don't use a calculator for this sheet

1 Write in the missing numbers:

a) double → double → double → double
| 2.1 | → [ ] → [ ] → [ ] → [ ]

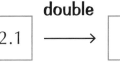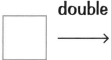

b) halve → halve → halve → halve
| 88.8 | → [ ] → [ ] → [ ] → [ ]

2 Elliot has been measuring the length of worms in his garden:

Worm A  Worm B 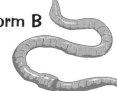 Worm C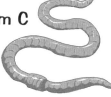

4.2 cm   **6.7** cm

a) The length of Worm C is double the length of Worm A. How long is it? Show your working.

b) Elliot finds another worm which is half the length of Worm B. How long is it? Show your working.

3 Sir Lancelot's sword is **92.4** cm long. King Arthur's is double that length. Complete the calculation below to show how long it is.

a) 92.4 + [ ] = [ ]

None shall pass.

b) Sir Mordred's short sword is half the length of Lancelot's sword. Complete the calculation below to show how long it is.

92.4 ÷ [ ] = [ ]

Activity Measure the length of a few things at home, such as your pencils or pencil case, in <u>cm</u> and <u>mm</u>. Now work out <u>double</u> and <u>half</u> of these lengths.

Learning Objective:

"I can double and halve using decimals."

© 2008 CGP

Doubling and Halving

Don't use a calculator for this sheet

1   Write in the missing numbers:

a)   3.0 $\xrightarrow{\text{halve}}$ ☐   b)   0.94 $\xrightarrow{\text{halve}}$ ☐

c)   ☐ $\xrightarrow{\text{halve}}$ 6.4   d)   ☐ $\xrightarrow{\text{halve}}$ 0.95

2   100 – 62 = 38. Use this to help you write a similar calculation to find the difference between 10.0 and 6.2.

3   Tom's dad says he will match whatever Tom saves towards buying a new computer game. Tom manages to save £18.50.

a)   With his dad's money too, does Tom have enough to buy a game that costs £35.00? Show how you know.

b)   A different game costs £42.00. How much more does Tom need to save to buy this one instead?

4   Draw lines to pair up boxes which make the same numbers:

double 2.1

6.6 ÷ 2

5.5 – 2.2

3.2 + 4.4

half of 8.4

2 × 3.8

Activity   How wide is your tv or radio? Can you write some calculations to show <u>half</u> and <u>double</u> this width?

Learning Objective:

"I can add and subtract to make halves or doubles of decimals."

© 2008 CGP

Name: .... Date: **57**

Factors and Multiples

1 | Circle the numbers which are factors of 24:

1   2   3   4   5   6
  7   8   9   10   11   12

Factors are the smaller whole numbers you get by dividing a bigger number exactly.

2 | Fill in the missing factors:

Use different numbers each time.

a) $\boxed{1} \times \boxed{12} = 12$

b) $\boxed{} \times \boxed{} = 12$

c) $\boxed{} \times \boxed{} = 12$

3 | Write down ALL the factors of the following numbers:

a) The factors of 15 are: ☐ ☐ ☐ ☐

b) The factors of 36 are: ○ ○ ○ ○ ○ ○ ○ ○ ○

4 | Circle the common multiples of **3** and **4**.

36   21   24   39
  40   15   20
30   10   18   12

Multiples are the bigger numbers you get by multiplying two smaller numbers.

Activity How many common multiples of 4 and 6 are there below 1000? You don't need to actually find them all to work out how many there are. Show how you worked this out. You can use a calculator.

Learning Objective:

"I can find pairs of factors of two-digit whole numbers and find common multiples (e.g. for 6 and 9)."

SHEET 1   © 2008 CGP

Factors and Multiples

1 | **Find all the factor pairs:**

a) ☐ × ☐ = 24   ☐ × ☐ = 24

☐ × ☐ = 24   ☐ × ☐ = 24

b) ☐ × ☐ = 38   ☐ × ☐ = 38

c) ☐ × ☐ = 17

2 | **Circle the common multiples of 3 and 5.**

12   15   20   25   30   33

36   40   45   50   60

3 | **Write down ALL the factors of the following numbers:**

a) The factors of 32 are:

b) The factors of 72 are:

c) The factors of 96 are:

4 | **Place these numbers in the correct part of the Venn diagram:**

105   153
145   180
210   225
243   374
360   315
405   306

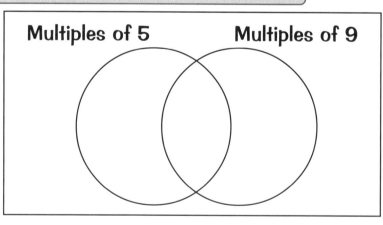

Multiples of 5   Multiples of 9

Activity   Lollipops cost 6p and gobstoppers cost 7p.
Alex wants to spend the same amount of money on each type
of sweet. How much could she spend on each of them?

Learning Objective:

"I can find pairs of factors of two-digit whole numbers and
find common multiples (e.g. for 6 and 9)."

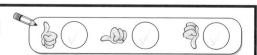

© 2008 CGP

Factors and Multiples

1 | Which of these numbers are prime numbers? Circle them:

98   19   31

83   13   27   65   53

79   26   39

Prime numbers only have two factors — 1 and themselves.

2 | Write down a factor pair for each number, and circle the correct option to say whether the number is prime or not.

a) 42 = ☐ × ☐

42 is prime / not prime.

b) 23 = ☐ × ☐

23 is prime / not prime.

c) 17 = ☐ × ☐

17 is prime / not prime.

d) 29 = ☐ × ☐

29 is prime / not prime.

3 | Write in the prime factors of these numbers:

a) 77 = ☐ × ☐

b) 12 = ☐ × ☐ × ☐

c) 18 = ☐ × ☐ × ☐

4 | Complete the following factor trees.

36

9   ☐

☐   ☐   ☐   ☐

210

10   ☐

☐   ☐   ☐   ☐

Activity What is the largest number you can make with only 3 different prime factors which are all less than 100? (you may need a calculator)

Learning Objective:

"I can find prime numbers up to 100.
I can find the prime factors of two-digit numbers."

© 2008 CGP

Multiplication and Division

1 | **Complete these calculations.**

a) $9 \times \boxed{} = 63$ d) $45 \div \boxed{} = 5$

b) $6 \times 9 = \boxed{}$ e) $48 \div 6 = \boxed{}$

c) $\boxed{} \times 4 = 32$ f) $56 \div 7 = \boxed{}$

2 | **Solve these problems. Show your working.**

a) Twenty-one sprouts are shared between some children.
Each gets five and there is one left over. How many children are there?

b) Bill gives four rollerskates to each of his six zebras. He has
three rollerskates left over. How many rollerskates did he have?

c) Sam has six books. They each have six pages. He reads four pages a
night. How many nights will it take him to finish all the books?

3 | **Find the mystery numbers.**

a) I am a multiple of both 8 and 6. I am less than 30.

b) If you multiply me by 10 then divide me by 4 you get 5.

Activity Find 5 numbers less than 20 that can only
be divided exactly by themselves and 1.
E.g. 7 can only be divided by 1 and 7.
It can't be divided by 2, 3, 4, 5 or 6.

In other words, ones
that aren't multiples of
any other numbers.

Learning Objective:

"I know all my multiplication and division facts up to
10×10. I can spot multiples of numbers up to 10."

       © 2008 CGP

Multiplication and Division

Don't use a calculator for this sheet

1 | **Work out each division, then complete the multiplication underneath.**

a) $24 \div 6 = \boxed{}$ **b)** $63 \div 7 = \boxed{}$ **c)** $32 \div 8 = \boxed{}$

$\boxed{} \times 6 = 24$ $\boxed{} \times 7 = 63$ $\boxed{} \times \boxed{} = 32$

2 | **Work out these multiplications.**

a) $20 \times 4 = \boxed{}$ **b)** $200 \times 4 = \boxed{}$

c) $3 \times 60 = \boxed{}$ **d)** $3 \times 600 = \boxed{}$

3 | **Work out these divisions.**

Check your answers by multiplying.

a) $120 \div 4 = \boxed{}$ **b)** $2100 \div 30 = \boxed{}$

c) $250 \div 50 = \boxed{}$ **d)** $280 \div 70 = \boxed{}$

4 | **Write the numbers below in the correct box.**

Some numbers go in more than one box.

60   120   150   160   200   240

Multiples of 20	Multiples of 30	Multiples of 40	Multiples of 50

Activity   Find as many multiplications and divisions as you can that give an answer between 30 and 40.

Learning Objective:

"I can use tables facts to multiply multiples of 10 and 100 and to find linked division facts."

SHEET *8*   © 2008 CGP

Multiplication and Division

Don't use
a calculator
for this sheet

1 Try to divide each number down the side of this grid by the numbers across the top. If it won't divide exactly put an **X**.

	÷2	÷3	÷4	÷5	÷6	÷7	÷8	÷9	÷10
24	12	8	6	X	4	X	3	X	X
36									
35									
48									
56									

2 Work out these multiplications.

a) $3 \times 6 = $ ☐

b) $7 \times 4 = $ ☐

c) $8 \times 5 = $ ☐

d) $9 \times 6 = $ ☐

e) $7 \times 8 = $ ☐

f) $8 \times 6 = $ ☐

3 Now try these:

Use your answers to question 2 to help you work these out.

a) $30 \times 6 = $ ☐

b) $7 \times 40 = $ ☐

c) $80 \times 5 = $ ☐

d) $90 \times 60 = $ ☐

e) $70 \times 80 = $ ☐

f) $80 \times 60 = $ ☐

Activity

Barry Davies says his lucky number is 3 because his first name has 5 letters and his second name has 6 letters. When 5 and 6 are multiplied together they make 30. And when you add the digits in 30 together (3 + 0) you get 3. Use the same system to work out your lucky number. Who do you know that would have the highest lucky number?

Learning Objective:

"I can use tables facts to multiply multiples of 10 and 100 and to find linked division facts."

© 2008 CGP

Key Objective

Multiplication and Division

Don't use a calculator for this sheet

1 | Work out these multiplications.

a) $0.6 \times 5 =$ ☐ b) $8 \times 0.7 =$ ☐ c) $0.5 \times 5 =$ ☐

d) $0.7 \times 4 =$ ☐ e) $7 \times 0.4 =$ ☐ f) $0.3 \times 8 =$ ☐

2 | Work out these divisions.

a) $3.6 \div 6 =$ ☐ b) $5.4 \div 9 =$ ☐ c) $3.5 \div 5 =$ ☐

d) $4.9 \div 7 =$ ☐ e) $2.4 \div 4 =$ ☐ f) $2.8 \div 4 =$ ☐

3 | Write the correct number in each box.

a)
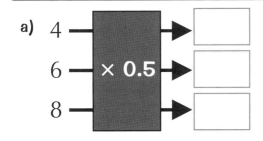

b)
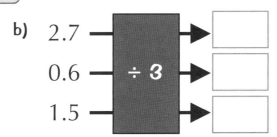

4 | Mary had a little lamb. Its fleece was white as snow. So she sheared it and sold the fleece for £4.20.

a) She had to share the profit between herself and her 6 brothers. How much did Mary get?

b) Her father decided to sell the fleeces from his 9 sheep. He only got £0.90 for each fleece. How much did he get altogether?

Activity £4.20 can be shared equally between a group of 7 people. What other size groups of people can £4.20 be equally shared between?

Try groups of between 1 and 20 people.

Learning Objective:

"I can use tables facts to work out related facts with decimals."

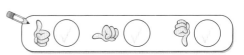

  © 2008 CGP

Calculators

1 | Use a calculator to work these out:

a) $652 \times 71 =$ ▢

b) $3861 \div 27 =$ ▢

c) $437 \times 58 =$ ▢

d) $7 + 131 + 782 =$ ▢

e) $737 + 17 - 57 =$ ▢

f) $3617 - 7762 =$ ▢

2 | Lindsey has £14. She shares it equally between herself and 4 friends.

Using your calculator, work out how much money they will each get.

▢

3 | Calculate the answers to these money problems:

a) $£1.70 - 48p =$ ▢

b) $£7.32 \div 6 =$ ▢

c) $£4.74 \div 6 =$ ▢

d) $£87 - £2.92 =$ ▢

e) $96p + £1.03 =$ ▢

f) $£13.10 \times 12 =$ ▢

4 | Try these questions involving negative numbers:

a) $-2 \times 71 =$ ▢

b) $-27 \div 3 =$ ▢

c) $-52 + 131 =$ ▢

d) $-5 \times -3 =$ ▢

5 | My piggy bank has £10.92 in it. If I take 13p out every day for sweets, how many weeks will it take for me to empty it?

▢

Activity Find some <u>adverts</u> in a newspaper that are <u>selling things</u>. Try to find <u>5 objects</u> which have prices that add up to £30.

Learning Objective:

"I can use my calculator to work out problems involving money and negative numbers."

© 2008 CGP

Calculators

1 | Use a calculator to work out the following problems:

a) $1.3 \times 1.3 =$ ☐

c) $75 \div 12 =$ ☐

b) $125 \div 4 =$ ☐

d) $13.5 - 8.05 =$ ☐

2 | Find the answers to these fractions using your calculator:

a) $\frac{1}{4}$ of $272 =$ ☐

e) $\frac{1}{8}$ of $176 =$ ☐

b) $\frac{3}{4}$ of $272 =$ ☐

f) $\frac{5}{8}$ of $176 =$ ☐

c) $\frac{1}{5}$ of $395 =$ ☐

g) $\frac{1}{12}$ of $252 =$ ☐

d) $\frac{3}{5}$ of $395 =$ ☐

h) $\frac{7}{12}$ of $252 =$ ☐

3 | Lisa owns a pencil factory. One pencil is **13.2** cm long.

a) How long would a line of **75** pencils be? ☐

b) How many centimetres less than 10 metres is this? ☐

4 | Calculate the answer to these problems. Give your answer in the most appropriate units (millimetres, centimetres, metres or kilometres).

a) $15.6 \text{ cm} \times 12 =$ ☐

d) $1.03 \text{ km} \div 36 =$ ☐

b) $15.6 \text{ m} \div 12 =$ ☐

e) $76 \text{ mm} \times 143 =$ ☐

c) $12.7 \text{ m} \times 923 =$ ☐

f) $12 \text{ mm} + 1.2 \text{ m} =$ ☐

Activity — Measure the length of your <u>stride</u> to the nearest centimetre. How far would you walk in <u>**2000**</u> steps? Or <u>**3000**</u> steps?

Learning Objective:

"I can calculate problems involving decimals or fractions."

© 2008 CGP

Calculators

1 | **Use a calculator to work out these equations:**

a) $1.6 \text{ kg} + 2.075 \text{ kg} =$ ☐

d) $3.1 \text{ kg} - 1.07 \text{ kg} =$ ☐

b) $8 \times 250 \text{ g} =$ ☐

e) $2.2 \text{ kg} - 1.7 \text{ kg} =$ ☐

c) $2.4 \text{ kg} \div 6 =$ ☐

2 | **Find the answers to these fractions using your calculator.**

a) $\dfrac{1}{4}$ of $1 =$ ☐

c) $\dfrac{5}{8}$ of $1648 =$ ☐

b) $\dfrac{3}{4}$ of $52 =$ ☐

d) $\dfrac{9}{16}$ of $1648 =$ ☐

3 | **Calculate these fractions and put the answers in the correct section:**

$\dfrac{1}{4}$ of 5.6kg $\dfrac{3}{4}$ of 2kg

$\dfrac{2}{5}$ of 2kg $\dfrac{7}{8}$ of 1.2kg

$\dfrac{8}{10}$ of 500g $\dfrac{7}{3}$ of 800g

$\dfrac{7}{31}$ of 10kg $\dfrac{3}{15}$ of 4.8kg

$\dfrac{3}{7}$ of 2kg $\dfrac{19}{20}$ of 1.1kg

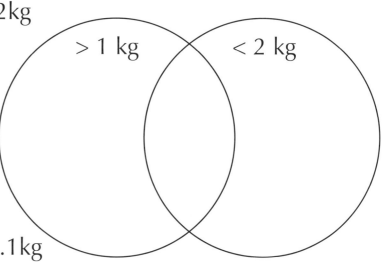

> 1 kg   < 2 kg

4 | **A bunch of 7 bananas's mass is 500 g. Rudolph eats 30 bananas a day.**

Work out the mass of bananas that Rudolph will eat in a day.

☐

 Activity   Measure your <u>arm span</u>. <u>Calculate</u> how many spans it would take to form a ring with a circumference of **168 m.**

Learning Objective:

"I can use my calculator to work out fractions."

          © 2008 CGP

Calculators

1 | Use a calculator to work out these problems:

    a) $12.5 \times 3.5 =$ ⬚

    b) $3.4 + 5.98 + 4.54 =$ ⬚

    c) $4.7 \times 3.43 \times 2.1 =$ ⬚

2 | Bill buys **27** goldfish which cost **6** pence each.

How much change does he get from a £2 coin? ⬚

3 | Place these fractions in the correct places on the number line.

$\dfrac{3}{22}$ of 15 $\dfrac{1}{4}$ of 17 $\dfrac{3}{20}$ of 27 $\dfrac{4}{17}$ of 12

   $\dfrac{1}{6}$ of 23 $\dfrac{8}{35}$ of 11 $\dfrac{1}{15}$ of 52 $\dfrac{2}{8}$ of 9

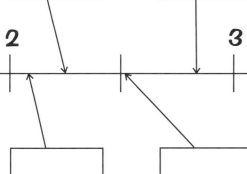
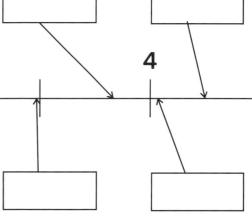

4 | In each class in St Mary's Primary School there are **12** boys and **16** girls. There are **156** boys in the school. How many girls are there altogether?

⬚

| Activity | Find three <u>telephone numbers</u>. For each one, add all the digits together and find the <u>average</u>. |

Learning Objective:

"I can use my calculator to solve problems involving fractions and decimals."

© 2008 CGP

Calculators

1 | **Silk costs £1.32 for 1 metre.** |

a)   How much would 2.7 metres cost?

b)   How many lengths of 1.8 metres can I cut from 43.2 metres?

2 | **Freddie wants to buy a new bike which costs £50. He saves £3.57 a week for a total of 13 weeks.** |

Work out how much more money he needs to buy the bike.

3 | **Calculate the answers to these problems:** |

a) $14 + (1 \times 2) =$

b) $18 + (7 \times 2) =$

c) $-7 + (77 \div 7) =$

d) $37 - (18 \times 13) =$

e) $46 - (27 \times 12) =$

When you use a calculator to solve these problems, it should use BODMAS. This stands for:

Brackets
Over
Division
Multiplication
Addition
Subtraction

You can use this order to work out which part of the equation to solve first.

4 | **Mike goes to watch a local football match with his friends.** |

The home side has 23,571 supporters and the away side has 12,452 supporters. 10 minutes from the end of the game, one quarter of the away supporters leave the stadium because they are losing the match. How many supporters are left at the stadium altogether at the end of the match?

| **Activity** | Use the bracket buttons on your calculator to do these calculations:

$2 \times (3 + 6)$ $(2 \times 3) + 6$

What happens if you just type in $2 \times 3 + 6$ without the <u>brackets</u>?
Try out some more calculations with the brackets in different places.

Learning Objective:

"I can use my calculator to solve problems that have more than one part and involve brackets."

SHEET 6   © 2008 CGP

Key Objective

Mental Maths

Don't use a calculator for this sheet

1 | Fill in the missing numbers.

a) $42 - \boxed{} = 30$ b) $28 + 36 = \boxed{}$

c) $\boxed{} + 72 = 100$ d) $15 + \boxed{} = 50$

e) $94 - 82 = \boxed{}$ f) $\boxed{} - 31 = 8$

2 | Circle the pairs that have a difference of 12.

37 and 50   41 and 29   74 and 82

15 and 17   58 and 36   25 and 37

3 | Use rounding and adjusting to complete these sums.

Round one or both numbers to the nearest 10, then adjust at the end.
Then show what you did to work them out.

a) $19 + 35 = \boxed{}$ What I did: $\boxed{}$

b) $31 + 17 = \boxed{}$ What I did: $\boxed{}$

c) $78 + 20 = \boxed{}$ What I did: $\boxed{}$

4 | Now try these questions:

a) I have 43p and Bob has 36p.
    How much more money do I have than Bob? $\boxed{}$

b) I have completed 43 skips.
    How many more do I need to do before I reach 100? $\boxed{}$

Activity   Choose a list of numbers out of the phone book. See if you can add the last two digits of some of them to get as close as you can to 100 without going over.

Learning Objective:

"I can add and subtract two two-digit numbers in my head."

© 2008 CGP

Mental Maths

Don't use a calculator for this sheet

1 | Use the times tables you know to work these out.

Explain how you did them.

a) $12 \times 9 =$ | 108 — I added 9×10 to $9 \times 2 = 90 + 18 = 108$

b) $20 \times 3 =$

c) $50 \times 5 =$

2 | Use your rounding skills to help do these calculations. Explain how you did them.

a) $5030 - 2997 =$

b) $2003 - 900 =$

3 | Solve these problems. Use jottings to help you.

a) One lolly costs 15p. How much would five cost?

b) Four apples cost 68p. How much would one cost?

c) I have 24p, but my friend has 4 times as much.
How much money does she have?

4 | Work out each answer in your head.   Explain how you did them.

a) $11 \times 25 =$

b) $2834 + 2999 =$

c) $14 \times 4 =$

Activity   Find 3 consecutive numbers that add up to 162
(consecutive means one after another, e.g. 2, 3, 4).

Learning Objective:

"I can multiply one and two digit numbers, and add and subtract numbers near to whole thousands in my head."

© 2008 CGP

Mental Maths

Don't use a calculator for this sheet

1 | Complete these calculations:

a) $3 \times 7 = \boxed{}$ b) $30 \times 7 = \boxed{}$ c) $0.3 \times 7 = \boxed{}$

d) $2 \times 8 = \boxed{}$ e) $20 \times 8 = \boxed{}$ f) $0.2 \times 8 = \boxed{}$

g) $6 \times 7 = \boxed{}$ h) $60 \times 7 = \boxed{}$ i) $0.6 \times 7 = \boxed{}$

2 | At a football match I bought a programme and two cups of coffee.

In total I spent five pounds. The programme was £2.60.

How much was one cup of coffee? $\boxed{}$

3 | Circle the two numbers that add up to 10.

9.09   0.01

9.99

9.9

0.11   1.01

4 | A piece of string is 3.6 m long.

a) If I cut it into 4 equal pieces, how long will each piece be? $\boxed{}$

b) If I cut it into 6 equal pieces, how long will each piece be? $\boxed{}$

c) If I cut off two pieces of 1.1 m each, how much will be left? $\boxed{}$

5 | What is 6.7 multiplied by 6?   Do it in your head, but write down how you worked it out.

$\boxed{}$

Activity Using the five numbers 250, 2, 3, 4, 5 and any of the four operations ($+$, $-$, $\times$, $\div$), what is the closest you can get to 517? You can use each number once.

Learning Objective:

"I can add, subtract, divide and multiply numbers with tens, units and tenths."

Multiply by 10, 100 and 1000

Don't use a calculator for this sheet

1 | **What is eight hundred and forty divided by ten?**

2 | **Fill in the missing numbers.**

100 kg   100 kg

a) $17 \times \boxed{} = 1700$

b) $\boxed{} \div 10 = 157$

c) $100 \times \boxed{} = 2300$

d) $3600 \div \boxed{} = 36$

3 | **Work out the answers to these problems:**

a) What number is 100 times bigger than 45?

b) What number is 10 times smaller than 5620?

c) What number is 10 times bigger than 27?

d) What number is 100 times smaller than 8600?

4 | **Stickers are sold in sheets of 10.**

I need six hundred and eighty stickers. How many sheets must I buy?

Activity | $60 \times 7 = 420$ is based on $6 \times 7 = 42$. List three other <u>multiplications</u> based on $6 \times 7 = 42$ and work out the answer to each. Now do the same with $3 \times 8 = 24$.

Learning Objective:

"I can multiply and divide numbers by 10 and 100."

© 2008 CGP

Multiply by 10, 100 and 1000

Don't use a calculator for this sheet

1 | Answer these questions:

a) How many tens are there in one hundred?

b) How many hundreds are there in one thousand?

c) How many tens are there in one thousand?

2 | Fill in the missing numbers.

a) $25 \times 10 = $

b) $5400 \div $ $= 5.4$

c) $420 \div $ $= 100$

d) $56.4 \times 10 = $

e) $73.6 \times 100 = $

f) $17.8 \div $ $= 1.78$

g) $\times 1000 = 16\ 000$

3 | Katie puts 100 2p coins edge to edge across a playground.

Each coin is 2.5 cm wide. How long is the line of coins?

4 | Greg is thinking of a number.

He divides the number by 100 and then by 10. His answer is 61.
What number was he thinking of? Show your working.

61...610...

Activity | Find a simple cake recipe. Calculate how much of each ingredient you would need to make a <u>hundred</u> cakes. How much would you need to make one <u>tenth</u> of one cake?

Learning Objective:

"I can multiply and divide decimals by 10, 100 and 1000."

  © 2008 CGP

Multiply by 10, 100 and 1000

Don't use a calculator for this sheet

1 | Match each number card to a calculation and write it in the correct box.

a) $4.3 \times \boxed{} = 430$

b) $72 \div \boxed{} = 7.2$

c) $6.5 \times \boxed{} = 6500$

2 | Calculate:

a) $75 \times 100 =$

b) $240 \div 2.4 =$

c) $2.1 \times 10 =$

d) $8.2 \div 10 =$

3 | How many hundreds are there in four thousand six hundred?

4 | Farmer Brown has 100 giant chickens.

He uses 73 kg of corn each day. Each chicken eats an equal amount.

a) How much corn does each chicken eat?

b) How much corn would the farmer need to feed 110 chickens?

Activity

Choose a 2-digit number. <u>Multiply</u> your number by 10. Now <u>divide</u> your original number by 10. Add the two numbers together. What do you notice? Try it with other numbers.

Learning Objective:

"I can multiply and divide numbers by 10, 100 and 1000 in my head."

© 2008 CGP

Using Fractions

Don't use a calculator for this sheet

1 | 30 guests are at a party. $\frac{1}{5}$ of the guests are boys. $\frac{4}{5}$ are girls.

How many boys and girls are there? ☐ boys ☐ girls

2 | Calculate these fractions.

a) $\frac{3}{8}$ of 24 g = ☐

b) $\frac{2}{7}$ of 21 cm = ☐

3 | A basketball team scores 32 points in a game.

Jason scores $\frac{1}{4}$ of the points.
Joanne scores $\frac{5}{8}$ of the points
and Lee scores $\frac{1}{8}$ of the points.

Complete the points chart. ⟹

Player	Jason	Joanne	Lee
Points scored	8		

4 | Elton has 50p. He spends $\frac{1}{10}$ of his money on sweets, $\frac{1}{5}$ on a pencil, $\frac{3}{10}$ on stickers and $\frac{2}{5}$ on a comic. How much does each item cost?

Sweets: ☐ p Pencil: ☐ p Stickers: ☐ p Comic: ☐ p

Activity | Write some fraction sentences about things you find in your house. For example:
$\frac{3}{8}$ of the rooms contain beds. $\frac{2}{5}$ of the toothbrushes are blue.

Learning Objective:

"I can find a fraction of a number or an amount."

© 2008 CGP

Name: ....   Date: ....

Using Fractions

Don't use
a calculator
for this sheet

1 | Work out these fractions. |

a) $\frac{2}{3}$ of 120 = [   ]

b) $\frac{7}{10}$ of 120 = [   ]

2 | Professor Digit's Number Machine can find 5% of any number. |

It has already worked out
5% of 20.
What answer will it give for the
other numbers? Write your
answers in the correct shapes.

*Remember that
5% is half of 10%*

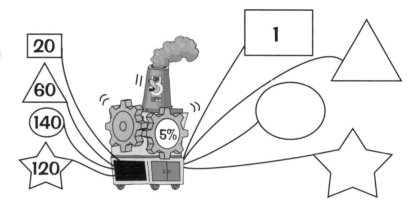

20
60
140
120
1
5%

3 | Fill in the gaps in the table. Show your working in the box below. |

Whole amount	20 m	40 kg	80 mins	£1.20
$\frac{3}{5}$				72 p
25%	5 m			

[   ]

| Activity | Find one fifth of each of these numbers: 35   100   75   150   60.
Which ones give answers of 15 or less?
Find 3 other numbers where the value of $\frac{1}{5}$ is a whole number that is
less than 15.

Learning Objective:

"I can find a fraction or percentage of an amount."

                                                        © 2008 CGP

Using Fractions

Don't use a calculator unless the question tells you to

1 | Fill in the missing numbers in the following number sentences.

a) $12 \div 3 = \dfrac{1}{\boxed{}}$ of 12

b) $18 \times \dfrac{1}{6} = 18 \div \boxed{}$

2 | Mary, Usha, Richard and Alex have ordered 5 pizzas.

How much pizza will they each get if they share the 5 pizzas equally?

$\boxed{}$

$\dfrac{\boxed{}}{\boxed{}}$ pizzas

3 | Complete the following table:

Calculation	27 ÷ 5	39 ÷ 4	58 ÷ 5	63 ÷ 10	
Fraction	$5\frac{2}{5}$				$3\frac{1}{4}$
Decimal	5.4				

4 | Draw lines to match the questions with the correct answers:

$\boxed{\dfrac{7}{8} \text{ of } 64}$ $\boxed{90\% \text{ of } 60}$ $\boxed{\dfrac{5}{11} \text{ of } 121}$

Dough!

52
   53
54
   55
56
    57

5 | Calculate the following:

a) 55% of 120 m = $\boxed{}$

b) 70% of 230 g = $\boxed{}$

Activity

Look for whole numbers in a magazine, newspaper or catalogue. Find 15%, 35%, and 65% of these numbers, writing your answers as decimals. Now find $\dfrac{4}{5}$, $\dfrac{3}{8}$ and $\dfrac{7}{10}$ of the numbers, writing your answers as fractions. <u>You can use a calculator.</u>

Learning Objective:

"I can find fractions and percentages of whole numbers."

© 2008 CGP

<u>Written Adding and Subtracting</u>

1 | Write the totals: |

a)   442
   + 233
   [ ]

b)   714
   + 125
   [ ]

c)   173
   + 418
   [ ]

2 | James got **845** points in a quiz. Oliver got **386** points.
How many more points did James get than Oliver? Show your working. |

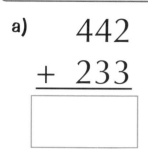

3 | Find the total cost of a bat costing **£2.25**, a ball costing **12p**
and a net costing **£1.95**. Show your working. |

4 | Fill in the missing digits. |

a) 24[ ] + 1[ ]4 = 400

b) [ ]42 − 23[ ] = 705

c) 1[ ]4 + 39[ ] = 528

d) [ ]87 − 1[ ]6 = 661

| Activity | Using only **2** of the numbers <u>342</u>, <u>634</u> and <u>478</u>, what is
the <u>largest difference</u> and the <u>smallest total</u> you can make?
Choose <u>another</u> set of 3-digit numbers. Using only **2** of them,
what is the largest difference and the smallest total this time?

<u>Learning Objective:</u>

"I can add and subtract two-digit and three-digit
numbers using a written method."

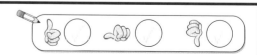

© 2008 CGP

Key Objective # Written Adding and Subtracting

1 | Calculate: |

a) 225
+ 169

b) 2.46
+ 1.73

c) 546
− 174

d) 174.7
− 30.8

2 | Calculate, showing your working clearly: |

a) 1.07 + 2.85

b) 27.8 − 2.5

c) 83.6 + 2.19

3 Rosie has £27.16 in her piggy bank.
She is given the same amount again.

How much does she now have in her piggy bank?

4 Mrs Coates is building cupboards. She has a bag of 300 nails.
One cupboard will need 84 nails and the other will need 198 nails.

How many nails will Mrs Coates have left over?

| Activity | Put numbers in the boxes to make this sum correct:

☐0 + ☐0 = 1☐0

How many other solutions can you find? Write them down.

Learning Objective:

"I can add and subtract whole numbers and decimals
with up to two places."

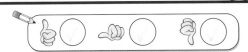

© 2008 CGP

Key Objective

Written Adding and Subtracting

1 | Each block is the total of the two blocks below it. |

Example:
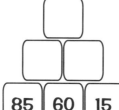

Complete these blocks in the same way.

a)
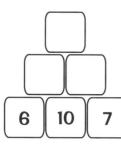

b)
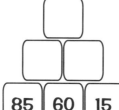

c)
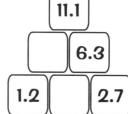

d)

2 | Find the difference between **28.31** and **15.06**. |

3 | Calculate, showing your working clearly: |

   a) $37 + 425 + 505$ **b)** $105 + 20 + 235$ **c)** $789 + 52 + 17$

4 | Three numbers total **172**. One of the numbers is **96** and another is **25**. |

What is the third number?

Activity
Find three different multiples of 5 with a total of 150.
Now find three numbers that aren't multiples of 5 with a total of 150.
Write down four more sets of three numbers that total 150.

Learning Objective:

"I can add and subtract whole numbers and decimals with up to two places."

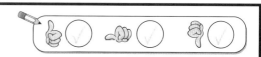

© 2008 CGP

Written Adding and Subtracting

Key Objective

1 | Calculate: |

a)   347
   + 289

b)   7.46
   + 5.83

c)   2059
   − 827

d)   62.01
   + 28.96

2 | Find the sum of 162.8, 25.7 and 309.4. |

3 | Fill in the missing numbers in these grids. |

The total of each line or column is written in the circle.

a)

25	30		(66)
50		26	(91)
	42	35	(93)
( )	(87)	( )	

b)

45	11	26	( )
	58		(108)
61		75	( )
(123)	(92)	(134)	

4 | Rachel got a new book at the weekend with 437 pages. |

She read 58 pages on Saturday, 93 pages on Sunday and 14 pages before school on Monday. How many pages does she have left to read?

| Activity | Find 3 books and write down the number of pages in each book.
Then find the total number of pages in all 3 books.
Find the total number of pages in 3 longer books.

Learning Objective:

"I can add and subtract whole numbers and decimals using efficient written methods."

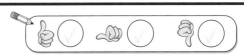

Key Objective

Written Multiplying and Dividing

1 Complete these calculations.

a) 26 × 4

×	4
20	80
6	24

b) 74 × 5

×	5
70	
4	

c) 57 × 3

×	

2 Complete these divisions.

Example: 85 ÷ 3

85 ÷ 3
= [60 ÷ 3] + [25 ÷ 3]
=   20   +   8 r1
=   <u>28 r1</u>

a) 79 ÷ 5

= [50 ÷ 5] + [   ]

= [   ] + [   ]

= [   ]

b) 81 ÷ 6

= [   ] + [   ]

= [   ] + [   ]

= [   ]

3 Solve these problems. Show your working for each.

a) Billy buys 6 pens for 96p.
How much is one pen?

b) Katie swims 9 lengths of a 25 m pool.
How far did she swim altogether?

Activity Look at this division: 74 ÷ 8 = 9 r 2. Think up two situations that could be solved with this division. Try to find one where the answer is rounded down to 9 and one where it's rounded up to 10.

Learning Objective:

"I can multiply and divide two-digit numbers and understand how to deal with the remainder."

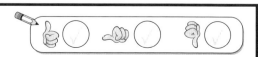

© 2008 CGP

Written Multiplying and Dividing

1 | Complete these multiplications. Fill in all the empty boxes. |

a)
$$345$$
$$\times \quad 8$$

$300 \times 8 =$

$40 \times 8 =$

$5 \times 8 =$

b)
$$14$$
$$\times \quad 26$$

$10 \times 26 =$

$4 \times 20 =$

$4 \times 6 =$

c) 5.3×9

2 | Solve the following problems. |

a) 928 cakes are put in boxes of 8. How many complete boxes can be made?

complete boxes

b) Four friends win £766 and split it evenly. How much do they each get, and how much is left? Show your working.

They get £   each.

There is £   left.

| Activity | Using only the digits 4, 5 and 6, write multiplications which give an answer that is less than 50. For example, 4.5 × 6 = 27.

Learning Objective:

"I can divide and multiply three-digit numbers and decimals."

 © 2008 CGP

Written Multiplying and Dividing

1 | **Complete these multiplications.** |

a)
$$724$$
$$\times\ 9$$

$700 \times 9 =$ ☐

$20 \times 9 =$ ☐

$4 \times 9 =$ ☐

☐

b)
$$53$$
$$\times\ 17$$

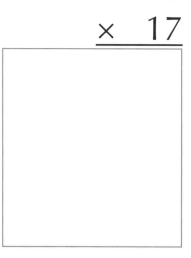

c) 36.8×9

2 | **Do each of these divisions and find the remainder.** |

Each remainder matches a letter in the table. One has been done for you. Put the letters you get together to spell a word.

Remainder	Letter
0	S
1	O
2	R
3	P
4	A
5	T
6	E

a) $5\overline{)643}$
   -600 (120 × 5)
   $\quad43$
   $-\ 40$ (8 × 5)
   $\quad\ 3$

   $120 + 8\ r3 = 128\ r3 \rightarrow$ **P**

b) $6\overline{)337}$

c) $4\overline{)928}$

d) $8\overline{)829}$

Word =

$\boxed{P\quad}$

Activity Multiply the age of the oldest member of your family by your age. Divide this number by how many people are in your family. Try dividing the number by a few other single digit numbers.

Learning Objective:

"I can do short division and I know how to break multiplications into steps to find the answer."

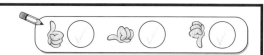

Written Multiplying and Dividing

Key Objective

1 | Do these divisions. |

    a) $9.9 \div 3$ b) $2375 \div 5$ c) $14.8 \div 4$

2 | Mario owns a pizza shop. Here is the menu: |

Pizza Menu

Cheese and Tomato £1.99
Ham and Mushroom £2.39
Pepperoni £2.99
Meat Feast £3.99
Bonanza (all toppings) £4.80

Garlic Bread....... £1.50
Chips.................. £1.00

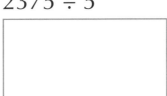

How much would it cost altogether to buy 6 Meat Feasts and 4 Garlic Breads?

3 | Find the answer to these problems. Write down your working. |

    a)   I choose a number and multiply it by 6.
            My answer is 103.2. What was my number?

    b)   Harry, Ali and Mukta are the same height.
            The total of their heights is 4.8 m. How tall is each person?

| Activity | Measure your height in centimetres. Now measure the length of your little finger in centimetres. Divide the first number by the second number. Do the same for 4 other people.

Learning Objective:

"I can divide and multiply numbers with decimals."

          © 2008 CGP

2D Shapes

1 | This picture is made from 2D shapes. Count the number of each type of shape and record it on the chart.

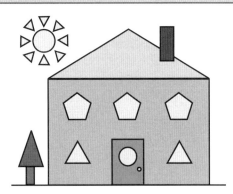

2D Shape	Number
Rectangles	
Triangles	
Pentagons	
Circles	

2 | For each shape, say how many sides and how many right angles it has:

a) Square   ☐ equal sides

☐ right angles

b) Equilateral ☐ equal sides
     Triangle

☐ right angles

c) Regular ☐ equal sides
     Pentagon

☐ right angles

3 | Draw these shapes on the grids below. Use a ruler.

a)

b)

c)

An isosceles triangle   A pentagon   A 4 sided shape with
(2 equal sides)   only two right angles

Activity | Look at the picture. These hexagons <u>tessellate</u> — they fit together with no gaps. Use squared paper to find three other shapes that tessellate.

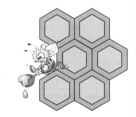

Learning Objective:

"I know facts about regular polygons such as the number of sides and number of angles."

    © 2008 CGP

2D Shapes

1 | Draw in the missing sides to create 3 rectangles. |

a)    b) 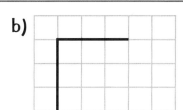   c)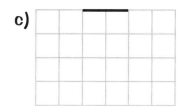

2 | Read the following sets of properties and use them to draw the shape being described. |

a) This shape has 5 lines of symmetry and no right angles.

b) This shape has 2 pairs of equal sides and no right angles.

c) This shape has 8 equal sides and no right angles.

3 | Here are some special types of triangle: |

An <u>equilateral triangle</u> has 3 equal sides and 3 equal angles.

An <u>isosceles triangle</u> has 2 equal sides and 2 equal angles.

A <u>scalene triangle</u> has 3 sides of different lengths.

A <u>right angled triangle</u> has 1 right angle.

Look at the following triangles and name them using the information given above.

a) 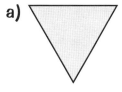   b) 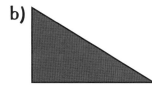   c) 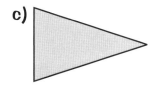   d)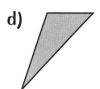

| Activity | Use a ruler to draw the four different types of triangle — label them with the correct names.

 Aaiee!

Learning Objective:

"I can describe the important features of 2D shapes."

© 2008 CGP

2D Shapes

1 **Look at the shapes below. Two of the edges have been dotted.**

Decide whether the dotted edges are parallel, perpendicular or neither.
Tick the boxes in the chart to show your answers.

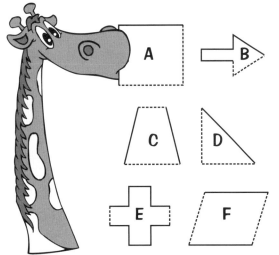

Shape	Perpendicular	Parallel	Neither
A			
B			
C			
D			
E			
F			

2 **Draw these shapes in the box. Write the name of the shape next to it.**

a) A 4 sided shape with 2 pairs of parallel sides — colour it green.
b) A 4 sided shape with only 1 pair of parallel sides — colour it red.
c) A 3 sided shape with 1 pair of perpendicular lines — colour it yellow.
d) A 6 sided shape with 3 pairs of parallel lines — colour it blue.

Activity   Design a spaceship, using a ruler to draw each part of it.
Try to include a trapezium, a hexagon and a right angled triangle.
Identify as many parallel and perpendicular lines as you can.

Learning Objective:

"I can classify 2-D shapes with perpendicular
or parallel sides."

                                          © 2008 CGP

3D Shapes

1 | Name the 3D shapes that are made from these nets.

a)

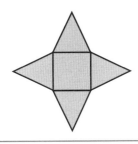

b)

c)

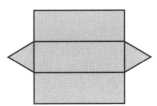

2 | Hamish links 5 cubes together.

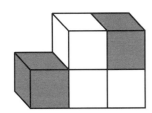

Hamish moves the shape. Shade in the black cubes on the shape in its new position.

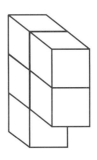

3 | Circle the nets that will fold up to make a cube.

a)

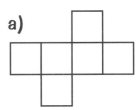

b)

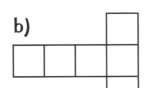

c)

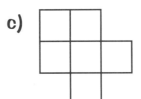

d)

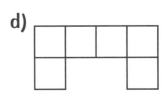

Activity Draw your own net for a cube. Make the sides of each square 5 cm long. Remember to include tabs so that you can stick the edges together. Cut out your net and fold it into a 3D cube.

Learning Objective:

"If I see a drawing of a 3D object I can visualise the solid shape. I recognise nets of 3D shapes."

© 2008 CGP

90   Name: ....   Date: ....

3D Shapes

1 | Circle the diagrams that show the net of a cuboid. |

a) 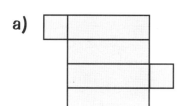   b) 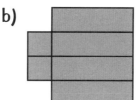   c) 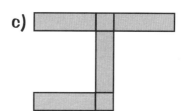   d)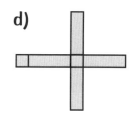

2 | Name the 3D shape, then draw its net. |

a)   4 vertices, 6 edges
and 4 faces.

3D shape: [   ]

Net:

b)   5 faces, made up of
rectangles and triangles.

3D shape: [   ]

Net:

3 | A square-based pyramid has 5
faces, 5 vertices and 8 edges. |  square

In the diagram below, 2 of these pyramids are
joined together. How many faces, edges and
vertices are there on the new shape?

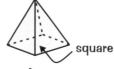

Faces: [ ]

Vertices: [ ]

Edges: [ ]

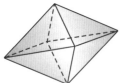 Activity   How many different ways can you draw a
net for this triangular prism?
Draw as many different nets as you can.

Learning Objective:

"I can identify 3D shapes and draw their nets."

SHEET 4   © 2008 CGP

3D Shapes

1 Complete these statements using the words <u>parallel</u> and <u>perpendicular</u>.

 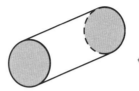 

a) The shaded faces of the cube are [   ] to each other.

b) The shaded faces of the cylinder are [   ] to each other.

c) The highlighted edges of the hexagonal prism are [   ] to each other.

2 Complete these statements by writing the correct numbers in the boxes.

a)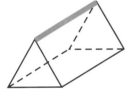

There are [ ] edges parallel to the shaded edge.

b)

There are [ ] faces perpendicular to the shaded face

c)

There are [ ] edges parallel to the shaded edge.

3 Name the 3D shapes Sam and Ayesha could be thinking of.

My shape has 3 pairs of parallel faces

My shape has 7 faces. 5 of them are perpendicular to the other 2.

Name of Sam's shape: [   ]

Name of Ayesha's shape: [   ]

Activity Draw the net of a cuboid on a separate piece of paper. Without folding the paper, colour in faces that will be parallel in the same colours. Mark edges that will be perpendicular with the same colours.

Learning Objective:

"I can use the properties of parallel and perpendicular to classify 3D shapes."

 © 2008 CGP

Name: .... Date: ....

Key Objective

Angles

1 | **Add the angles together in each of these diagrams.**

a)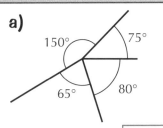

b)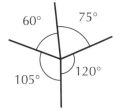

c)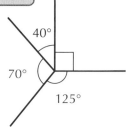

Angles add to [ ] °

Angles add to [ ] °

Angles add to [ ] °

Two of the diagrams are wrong.
Which ones? How do you know?

[ ]

2 | **Circle the greater angle in each pair below.**

a)

b)

c)

3 | **Put these angles in order of size.**

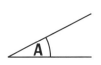

smallest [**B**] , [ ] , [ ] , [ ] , [ ] largest

4 | **Look at the following angles:**

Put a circle around the angle closest to 180°.
Put a square around the angle closest to 90°.

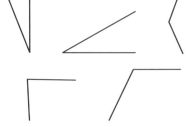

Activity

Draw a selection of angles (like in question 3).
Label them with letters, then put them in order of size.

Learning Objective:

"I know that one whole turn is 360°.
I can compare and order angles less than 180°."

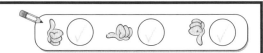

© 2008 CGP

Angles

1 | Estimate the following angles to the nearest 10°.

a)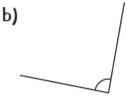

= ☐ °

b)

= ☐ °

c)

= ☐ °

2 | Measure each of the missing angles in the flowers below using a protractor.

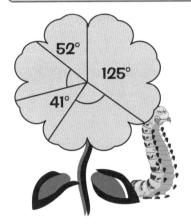

a) ☐ ° and ☐ °   b) ☐ ° and ☐ °   c) ☐ ° and ☐ °

3 | Using a protractor, draw the following angles.

65°   22°   137°

| Activity | Without using a protractor, draw the following angles by estimation. Then, using the protractor, measure each angle you have drawn and see how close you were. |

a) 90°   b) 45°   c) 150°   d) 22°   e) 178°

Learning Objective:

"I can estimate, draw and measure acute and obtuse angles using a protractor to a suitable degree of accuracy."

© 2008 CGP

Angles

1 **Measure angle 'x' in each triangles.**

Use a protractor.

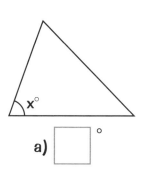 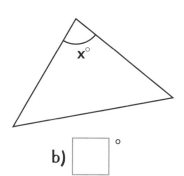 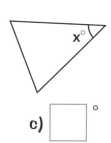

a) ☐°   b) ☐°   c) ☐°

2 **Look at these angles:**

 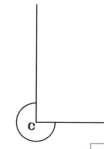 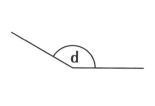

a) Write the letter of the angle that measures 150°: ☐

b) Write the letter of the angle that measures 310°: ☐

3 **Complete the drawings below to show the angles given.**

74°   132°   263°

Activity Draw a triangle. Measure two of its angles.
Angles in a triangle always add to 180°.
Use this to calculate the 3rd angle, then measure
it to check. Do the same with three different triangles.

Learning Objective:

"I can estimate angles and use a protractor to measure and
draw them, on their own and in shapes."

© 2008 CGP

Calculating Angles

1 | Barzan is swinging on a rope. What angle has he swung out to?

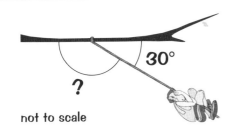

30°

?

not to scale

angle marked ? = [ ] °

2 | Calculate the missing angles in a) and b).

a)

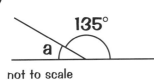

135°

a

not to scale

a = [ ] °

b)

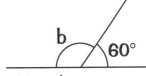

b

60°

not to scale

b = [ ] °

3 | Arran has drawn these three angles on a straight line:

Find the size of the missing angle.

angle marked ? = [ ] °

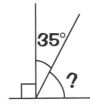

35°

?

not to scale

4 | Calculate the missing angles in a) and b).

a)

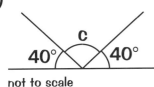

c

40°   40°

not to scale

c = [ ] °

b)

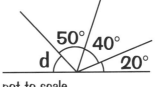

50° 40°

d   20°

not to scale

d = [ ] °

Activity

Using a ruler, draw a triangle and cut it out. Now tear off its corners.
Draw a straight line and try to fit the corners together along the line.
Do they fit together without gaps?
Try doing this with some different triangles.

Learning Objective:

"I can calculate angles on a straight line."

© 2008 CGP

Calculating Angles

1 | **Measure these angles using a protractor.**

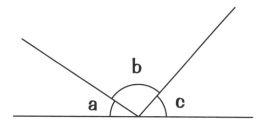

a = [ ]°   b = [ ]°   c = [ ]°

What do you notice about angles a, b and c?

[ ]

2 | **Lisa has half a cake left over from her birthday.**

She cuts it into six equal pieces.

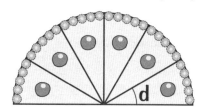

Calculate the size of angle d.
Show your working.

[ ]

3 | **A lamppost has been knocked over.**

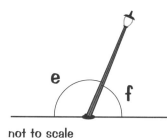

not to scale

Angle e is twice the size of angle f.
What size is angle e?

[ ]

Activity

How many different ways could you cut half a cake (180°) into equal pieces so that each piece is a whole number of degrees? For example, two slices are 90° each, three slices are 60°, and so on.

Learning Objective:

"I can calculate angles on a straight line."

SHEET 2

© 2008 CGP

Calculating Angles

1 | Find the missing angles in these triangles.

a)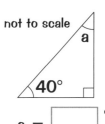
not to scale
a
40°

a = ☐ °

b)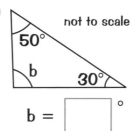
not to scale
50°
b
30°

b = ☐ °

c)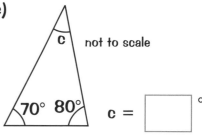
not to scale
c
70° 80°

c = ☐ °

2 | Find the missing angles in these isosceles triangles.

a)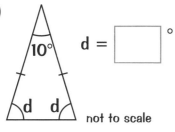
10°
d   d
not to scale

d = ☐ °

b)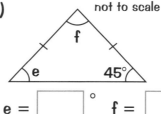
not to scale
f
e   45°

e = ☐ °   f = ☐ °

> Dashes on the sides of triangles mean the sides are the same length.

3 | A slice has been eaten from each of these pizzas.

Calculate the angles of the missing slices.

a)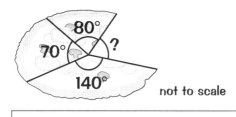
80°
70° ?
140°
not to scale

☐

b)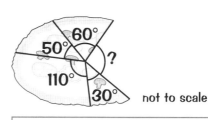
60°
50°
?
110°
30°
not to scale

☐

4 | This flower has five petals exactly the same size.

Calculate the angle that each petal makes around the centre.

☐

| Activity | Look at a clock face. Calculate the angle between the hour hand and the minute hand at 5 o'clock. Work out the angle between them at five different times. |

Learning Objective:

"I know that the angle sum of a triangle is 180° and the sum of angles around a point is 360°."

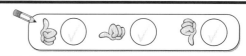

SHEET 3   © 2008 CGP

Coordinates

1 **Poppy is facing north-east.**

She turns through a half turn clockwise.
In what direction is she facing now?

[ ]

2 **Shade these squares on the grid:**

a) Shade C2, E1, C5, F1 and G2.

b) Shade the square half way
between A1 and G1.

c) Start at B1. Go 4 squares north and
5 squares east. Shade this square in.

3 **A dragon has kidnapped the princess.**

The knight wants to rescue her and get the dragon's treasure.
First he has to fight the dragon at Fire Mountain (in square C3).

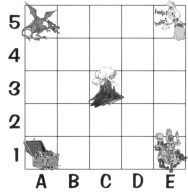

a) In what direction must the knight go to get
straight to Fire Mountain?

[ ]

b) In what direction must he go from
Fire Mountain to save the princess?

[ ]

c) Complete these directions to get from the princess to the treasure.

Go [ ] squares in a [ ] direction.

Activity Make up your own story like the one above.
Draw a map and write some questions to go with it.

Learning Objective:

"I can use the eight compass points."

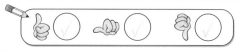

© 2008 CGP

Key Objective

Coordinates

1 | The map shows an island. |

The coordinates of 'Norton' are (10,7).

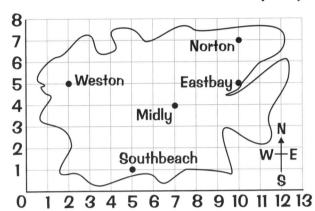

Write the coordinates of:

a) Weston

b) Midly

c) Eastbay

d) Southbeach

2 | Look at the grid below. |

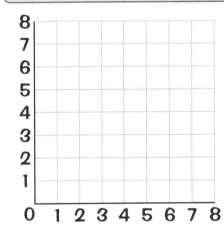

a) Plot these points on the grid:
(1,7), (5,7), (5,2), (1,2).

b) Join the points in order using straight lines. What shape have you drawn?

Use this grid to help you with question 3.

3 | Danny plots the points (2,6), (8,1) and (2,1) on a grid. |

He joins the points in order using straight lines. What shape has he drawn?

Activity The coordinates (2,5), (5,5), (5,2) and (2,2) are the vertices of a square. Write sets of coordinates that are the vertices of a scalene triangle and an isosceles triangle. Use squared paper to help you.

Learning Objective:

"I can read and plot coordinates to make shapes."

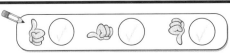

© 2008 CGP

Coordinates

1 **Three vertices of a parallelogram are at (2,1), (8,1) and (6,4).**

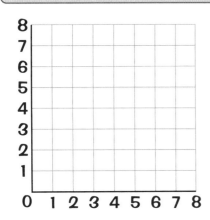

a) Plot these three points on the grid.

b) What are the coordinates of the fourth vertex of the parallelogram?

Use this grid to help you with question 3.

2 **Three _identical squares_ are plotted on the axes below.**

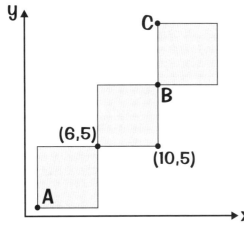

Find the coordinates of vertices A, B and C.

A:

B:

C:

3 **Siân plots these points on a set of axes: (4,1), (1,4), (4,7) and (7,4).**

She joins the points in order using straight lines. What shape has she drawn?

Activity Write coordinates for the vertices of a hexagon with:
a) 1 line of symmetry, b) 2 lines of symmetry.
Use squared paper to help you.

Learning Objective:

"I can use coordinates when the x-coordinate and the y-coordinate are both positive."

    © 2008 CGP

Drawing Shapes

1 Fill in the gaps in these sentences.

a) Horizontal lines go [   ] the page.

b) Vertical lines go [   ] the page.

2 Find all the horizontal lines in the picture below.

Go over the horizontal lines with a coloured pencil.

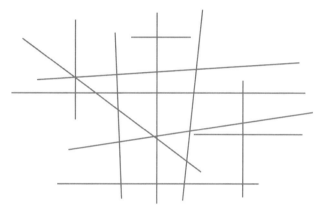

You might find a set-square helpful.

How many horizontal lines are there in the picture?

3 Now find all the vertical lines in the picture below.

Go over the vertical lines with a different coloured pencil.

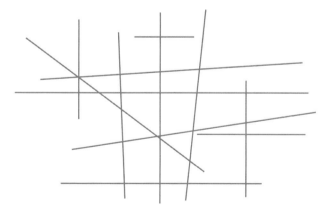

How many vertical lines are there in the picture?

Activity You can draw letters using only vertical and horizontal lines. Try writing your name this way.

Learning Objective:

"I know whether a line is horizontal or vertical."

© 2008 CGP

Key Objective

Drawing Shapes

1 | Tick the boxes under the sets of lines that are parallel to each other.

a) 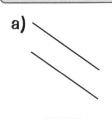 b) 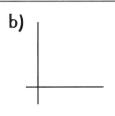 c) 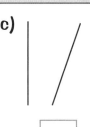 d) 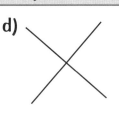 e)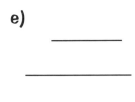

☐   ☐   ☐   ☐   ☐

2 | Which of these shapes have exactly two right angles?

 A   B  C D E

3 | Use a set-square and ruler to complete these shapes.

Start with the perpendicular lines.

a) A right-angled triangle with its two shorter sides both 4 cm long.

b) A square with 4 cm sides.

Activity

Plumb lines show if something is perpendicular to the ground. To make one you need a long piece of string (more than 50 cm) and a lump of Plasticine. Tie one end of the string to the Plasticine and make a loop for your finger at the other end. Hang the plumb line near a vertical line in your home, like a doorframe. If the frame is parallel to the string, then it is perpendicular to the ground.

Learning Objective:

"I can use a set-square and ruler to draw shapes with parallel and perpendicular sides."

  © 2008 CGP

Drawing Shapes

1 | This is an equilateral triangle. |

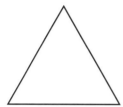

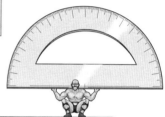

In the box, draw an accurate copy of the triangle <u>without tracing</u>. Use a ruler and protractor to help you.

2 | Using a ruler and protractor, draw a triangle with these properties. |

Longest side = 6 cm
Second side = 5.2 cm
Angle between them = 30°

Measure the length of the third side to the nearest millimetre.

3 | Use this shape to draw a pair of regular hexagons. |

Use a ruler and protractor.

| Activity | Look at the pattern below. Each new line has been drawn by increasing the angle between it and the line before by 10°. Continue the pattern. What happens after you get to 90°?

Use a ruler and protractor.

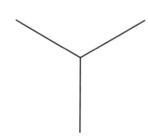

10°   20°   30°   40°

Learning Objective:

"I can make and draw shapes accurately."

© 2008 CGP

Symmetry

1 Draw **2** lines of symmetry on each of these shapes.

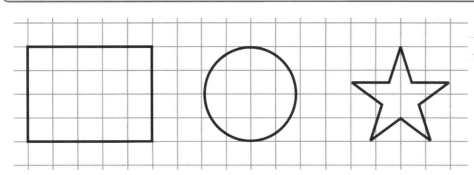

Use a mirror to help you spot lines of symmetry.

2 Complete the polygons below by filling in the other side of the line of symmetry.

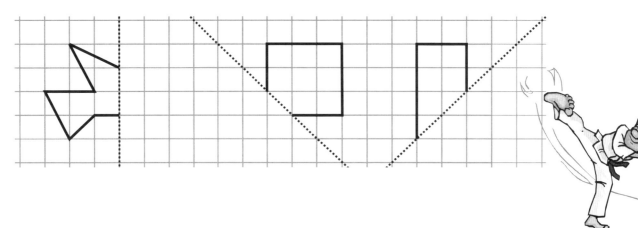

3 Draw lines of symmetry on these irregular polygons.

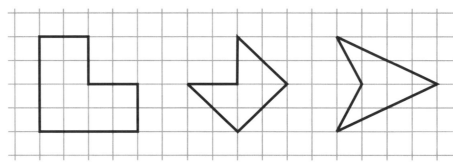

Activity Draw three irregular shapes on some squared paper. If you draw a line of symmetry along <u>one</u> of the <u>sides</u>, can you fill in the other side to make a <u>symmetrical</u> shape?

Learning Objective:

"I can recognise and draw symmetrical polygons."

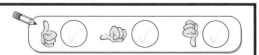

© 2008 CGP

Symmetry

1 | Draw two lines of symmetry on each of these patterns.

2 | Shade in the squares to make the patterns symmetrical about their lines of symmetry.

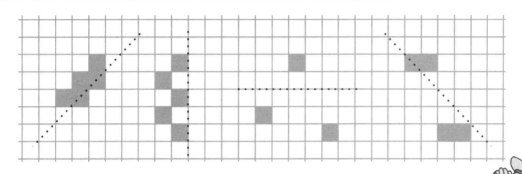

3 | Complete these patterns so that they are symmetrical about both lines of symmetry.

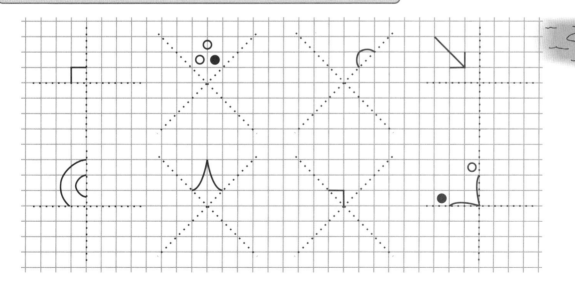

Activity | Using some squared paper to help, draw three patterns that all have at least <u>two</u> lines of <u>symmetry</u>.

Learning Objective:

"I can draw patterns with two lines of symmetry."

© 2008 CGP

Symmetry

1 Draw all the lines of symmetry on these shapes.
How many does each shape have? Write the number of lines
of symmetry and the name of the shape in the boxes below.

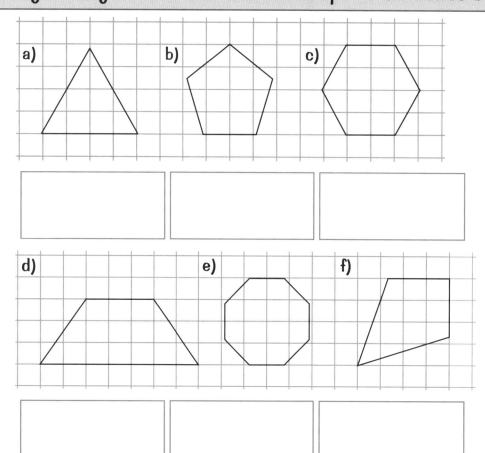

a)   b)   c)

d)   e)   f)

2 Shade in squares to make 2 different
shapes with 2 lines of symmetry each.
An example has been done for you.

Mmm...sausages.

Activity Draw some shapes with exactly 3, 4 and 5 lines of
symmetry. Can you find any shapes with even more?

Learning Objective:

"I can show every line of symmetry on 2-D shapes."

© 2008 CGP

Transformations

1 | **Reflect each shape in the mirror line.** |

a)

mirror line —————————

b)

mirror line —————————

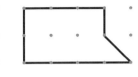

c)

mirror line

d)

mirror line

2 | **Look at the diagram below.** |

    a) Translate the square 3 units right and 2 units down.
    b) Translate the triangle 3 units left and 1 unit up.

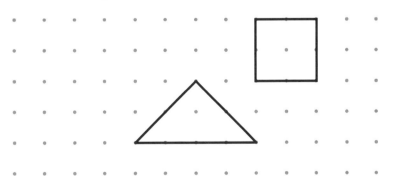

| **Activity** | On some grid paper, draw three <u>identical</u> squares.
Now, say how to <u>translate</u> the squares onto each other. |

Learning Objective:

"I can reflect and translate shapes."

Transformations

1 | **Reflect the shapes in the mirror lines.**

a)
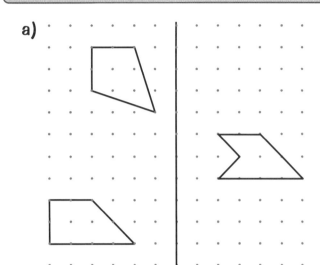
mirror line

b)
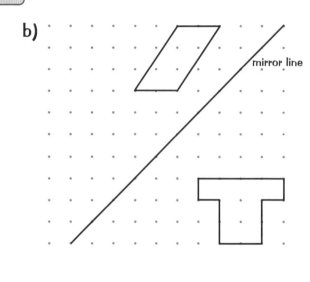
mirror line

2 | **Look at the diagram below.**

a) Translate shape A 6 units right and 1 unit up.
Do the same to the resulting shape.

b) Translate shape B 4 units left and 1 unit down.
Do the same to the resulting shape.

Activity — Label the two A shapes you have drawn above as A1 and A2.
Write down how to <u>translate</u> the original A to A2. Now try A2 to A1.

Learning Objective:

"I can reflect and translate shapes."

© 2008 CGP

Key Objective

Transformations

1 | Rotate these shapes 90° clockwise about the points shown.

a)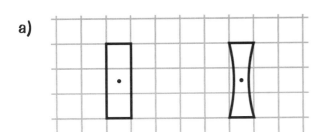

b)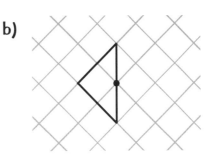

Rotate at 90°C

2 | Rotate each shape about the vertex shown.

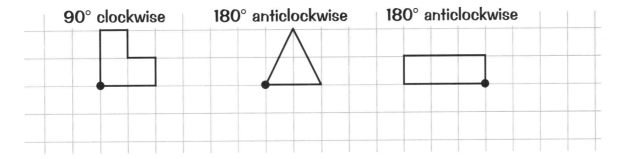

90° clockwise   180° anticlockwise   180° anticlockwise

3 | Follow the instructions to transform this shape.

a) Rotate 90° clockwise about the point shown.

b) Reflect the new shape in the mirror line.

c) Translate the new shape 4 units right and 2 units up.

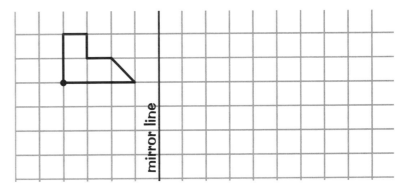

mirror line

Activity | <u>Rotate</u> this shape 180° clockwise about the point shown.

Can you find a way to do the same <u>transformation</u> using the mirror lines?

Will this work for any shape?

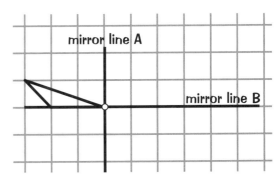

mirror line A

mirror line B

Learning Objective:

"I can reflect, translate and rotate shapes."

SHEET 3

© 2008 CGP

Calculating Perimeters and Areas

1 | **Draw rectangles with these perimeters:**

a) **12 cm**

b) **16 cm**

2 | **Find the perimeter of these posters. They aren't drawn to scale.**

a)
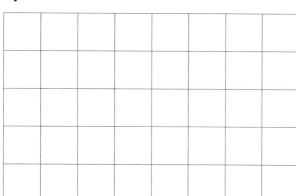
30 cm
40 cm

[ ] **cm**

b)

90 cm
50 cm

[ ] **cm**

3 | **Find the areas of these shapes.**

a)  b)

c) 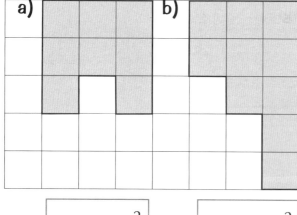 d)

[ ] **cm²**   [ ] **cm²**   [ ] **cm²**   [ ] **cm²**

Activity   Draw three different shapes that have the same area.

Learning Objective:

"I can draw a rectangle and work out its perimeter.
I can find the area of shapes by counting squares."

© 2008 CGP

Calculating Perimeters and Areas

1 | Measure the perimeters of these shapes:

a) 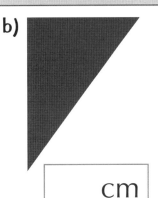   b)   c)    d)

| cm | | cm | | cm | | cm |

2 | Calculate the perimeters of these regular polygons:

a) 3 cm | cm |

b) 4 cm | cm |

c) 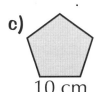 10 cm | cm |

d) 2 cm | cm |

3 | Use the formula <u>area = length × width</u> to calculate the areas of these rectangles:

a) 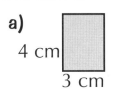 4 cm / 3 cm | cm² |

b) 5 cm  8 cm | cm² |

c) 9 cm 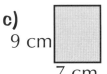 7 cm | cm² |

d) 2 cm 4 cm | cm² |

Activity — Draw four different rectangles with a perimeter of 20 cm. Calculate their areas. Are they all the same?

Learning Objective:

"I can measure the sides of polygons and find the perimeter. I can find the area of a rectangle using the formula."

SHEET **3**   © 2008 CGP

Calculating Perimeters and Areas

1 Calculate the perimeter and area of these shapes:

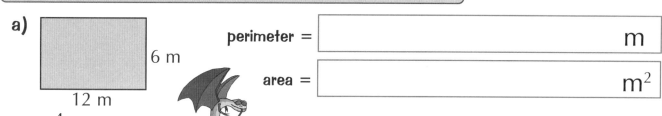

a)

6 m

12 m

perimeter = _____ m

area = _____ m²

b)

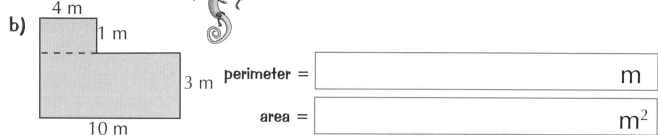

4 m

1 m

3 m

10 m

perimeter = _____ m

area = _____ m²

c)

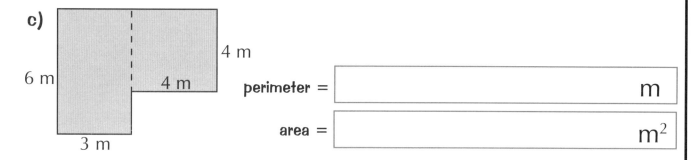

4 m

6 m

4 m

3 m

perimeter = _____ m

area = _____ m²

2 Estimate the areas of these shapes by counting the squares.

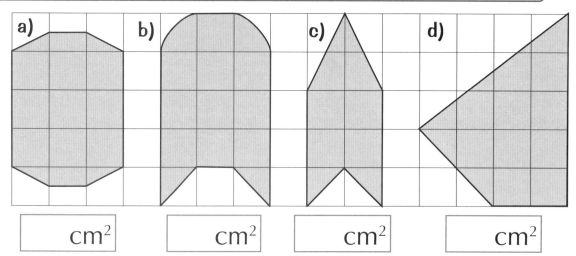

a)

b)

c)

d)

_____ cm²

_____ cm²

_____ cm²

_____ cm²

Activity Measure the length and width of a room at home.
Draw a diagram of it and calculate its perimeter and area.
You can use a calculator to work out the area.

Learning Objective:

"I can find the perimeter and area of shapes
and estimate the area of irregular shapes."

SHEET 4

© 2008 CGP

Drawing and Measuring

1 Complete the diagrams so that they become rectangles. Measure the perimeter of each rectangle.

a)

Perimeter =

cm

b)

Perimeter =

cm

c)

Perimeter =

cm

2 Draw rectangles of the correct sizes around the clowns. One corner has been drawn for you. Measure the perimeter of your rectangles.

a) Width = 4 cm
   Height = 3.5 cm

Perimeter =

cm

b) Width = 4.5 cm
   Height = 4 cm

Perimeter =

cm

c) Width = 3.5 cm
   Height = 3 cm

Perimeter =

cm

| Activity | Draw as many rectangles as you can that have a perimeter of 20 cm. The lengths of the sides can be whole or half centimetres. For example: Width 7 cm, length 3 cm. The perimeter is 3 cm + 7 cm + 3 cm + 7 cm = 20 cm. |

7 cm

3 cm

Learning Objective:

"I can draw a rectangle accurately and measure its perimeter."

© 2008 CGP

Key
Objective

Drawing and Measuring

1 | Measure these to the nearest millimetre. |

a)

Length = [   ] mm

b)

Width = [   ] mm

Length = [   ] mm

c)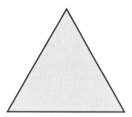

Length of each side =

[   ] mm

2 | James the ant has to carry leaves to six different places. |

His paths are shown by the dotted lines. Draw lines of the exact
lengths given to show how far he has to walk.

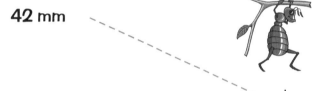

a)   42 mm

b)   27 mm

c)   35 mm

Start from here

d)   1.8 cm

e)   5.1 cm

f)   4.9 cm

3 | Meera has 2 identical boxes on her shelf. |

Draw a new box between
these 2 boxes so that
there is a 4 mm space
between each box. The
new box should be half
the height of the other 2.

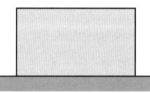 

Activity   Identify at least three things around your home that
measure between 221 mm and 247 mm. Record the items
and their measurements in a table.

Learning Objective:

"I can draw and measure lines to the nearest millimetre."

© 2008 CGP

Key Objective

Drawing and Measuring

1 | Isabelle is measuring her snails. The ruler is not drawn to scale. |

A

1cm 2 3 4 5 6 7 8 9 10

B

a) How long is snail A?

| | mm

b) How much longer is snail A than snail B?

| | mm

c) What is the distance between the end of snail A's tail and the end of snail B's tail?

| | mm

2 | Garp has drawn a plan of the 3 planets he wants to invade.
He can invade them in 6 different orders.
He starts from O, the dot in the middle. |

Use a ruler to measure the length of each possible route to the nearest millimetre.
The first one has been done for you.

a) OABC = distance between O and A
  + distance between A and B
  + distance between B and C
  = 107 mm

A

B

O ⊙

C

b) OACB =

c) OBAC =

d) OBCA =

e) OCAB =

f) OCBA =

Activity

Use a tape measure or a ruler to measure the height and width of one of the doors in your house. Suppose you had a set of rectangular postcards measuring 10 cm × 15 cm. How many postcards could you stick on to the door? Could you fit more on by sticking some sideways?

Learning Objective:

"I can read scales and use them to solve problems."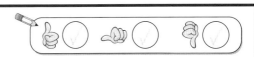

© 2008 CGP

Reading Scales

1 **What temperature is shown on each of these thermometers?**

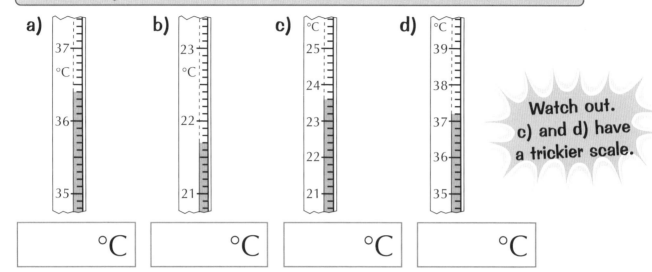

a) °C   b) °C   c) °C   d) °C

Watch out. c) and d) have a trickier scale.

2 **How much camel spit is in each jug?**

a) ml   b) ml   c) litres   d) litres

3 **Work out the mass of each dog.**

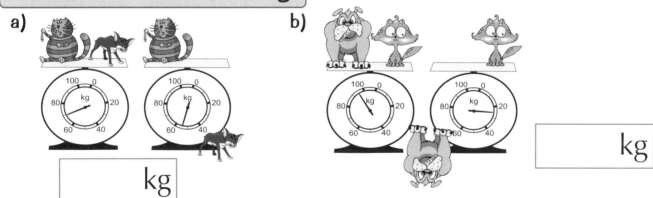

a) kg   b) kg

Activity Find four small containers, such as yoghurt pots and cups. Fill one of the containers with water, tip it into a measuring jug and read the scale. Do this with the other containers.

Learning Objective:

"I can read a scale to the nearest tenth of a unit."

© 2008 CGP

Reading Scales

1 Write the correct number in each box.

a)
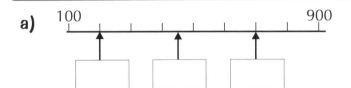

b)
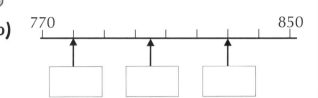

c) d)
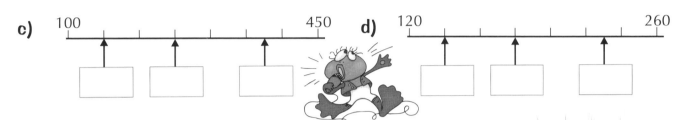

e)
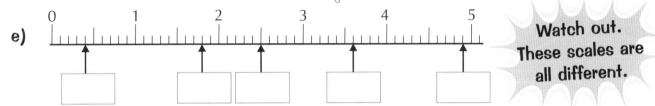

Watch out.
These scales are
all different.

f) g)
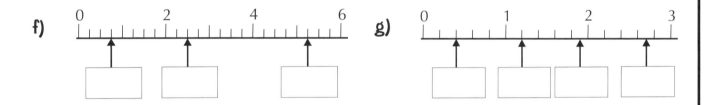

2 How much liquidised frog is in each jug?

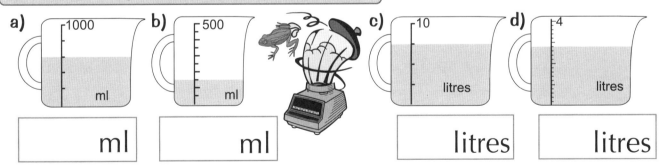

a) _____ ml   b) _____ ml   c) _____ litres   d) _____ litres

Activity Measure your height, mass and hand span.
You'll need to make sure you choose the right
measuring device and read the scale correctly.

Learning Objective:

"I can find the value of each interval on a scale so that
I can read measurements accurately."

© 2008 CGP

Reading Scales

1 | Write the temperature or shade in the mercury to complete these. |

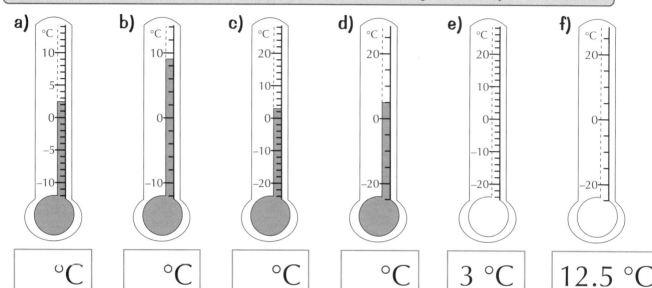

| a) | b) | c) | d) | e) | f) |

| °C | °C | °C | °C | 3 °C | 12.5 °C |

2 | This diagram shows the distances of different towns from Antville. |

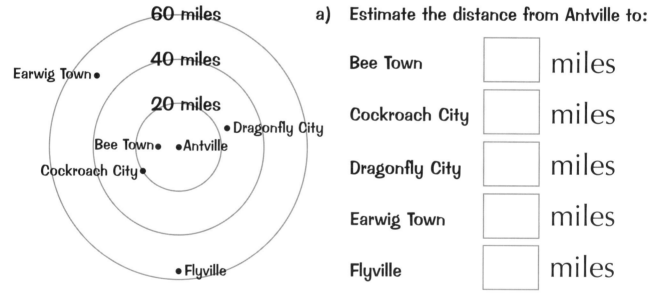

60 miles

40 miles

Earwig Town •

20 miles

• Dragonfly City

Bee Town •   • Antville

Cockroach City •

• Flyville

a) Estimate the distance from Antville to:

Bee Town [ ] miles

Cockroach City [ ] miles

Dragonfly City [ ] miles

Earwig Town [ ] miles

Flyville [ ] miles

b) Spider Town is 30 miles from Antville. Waspville is 45 miles from Antville. They are both in the same direction as Flyville. Mark these places on the map.

| Activity | Find out the distances of some places from the town where you live. Make a diagram, like the one above, showing how far away the places are. Choose your scale carefully. |

Learning Objective:

"I can find the value of each interval on a scale so that I can read measurements accurately."

   © 2008 CGP

Reading Scales

1 | **What is the difference between the readings on Scale A and Scale B?**

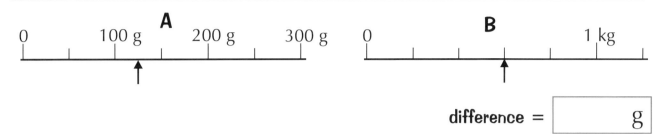

difference = ☐ g

2 | **Here are some things lined up on a scale.**

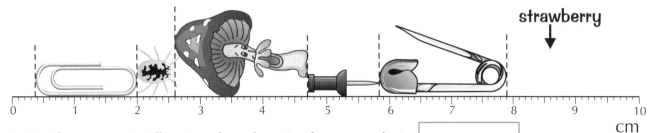

a)   To the nearest millimetre, how long is the paperclip?   ☐ mm

b)   To the nearest centimetre, how long is the toadstool?   ☐ cm

c)   How many millimetres longer than the insect is the toadstool?

☐ mm

d)   A strawberry is 12 mm long. Draw it on the scale so it just touches the safety pin.

3 | **Mark the mass of each item on the second set of scales.**

a)

b)

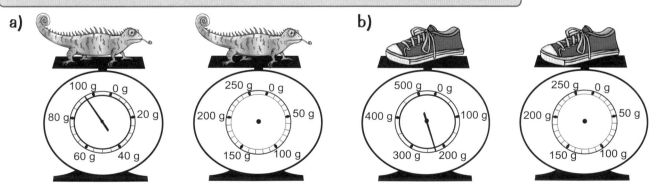

Activity   Measure the mass of some different items on some scales.
Copy both the scales in question 1 and
mark the masses of your items on each scale.

Learning Objective:

"I can read scales and give my answers as accurately as
the question asks."

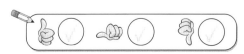

Time

1 | Fill in the missing times below.

a) 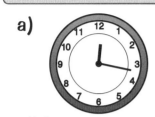 $\boxed{12:17}$

b)  $\boxed{10:56}$

c)  $\boxed{11:13}$

d) 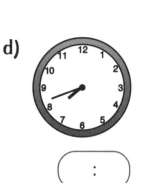 $\boxed{:}$

2 | What times will the watches below show in **47 minutes' time**? Write whether each time is am or pm.

a) $\boxed{11:23}$ am   b) $\boxed{11:48}$ pm   c) $\boxed{6:13}$ pm

$\boxed{:}$ $\boxed{:}$ $\boxed{:}$

3 | Answer the questions below using the best unit of time.

a) Ellen's birthday is on November 28th. How long does she have to wait until Christmas? $\boxed{}$

b) Dwain leaves Maths at 11.30 and 10 seconds. He gets to English at 11.31 and 4 seconds. How long did it take to get there? $\boxed{}$

4 | Use the train timetable to answer the questions below.

a) How long does it take to travel from London King's Cross to Exeter St Davids? $\boxed{}$

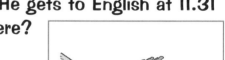

London King's Cross	10.50 am
Taunton	12.40 pm
Exeter St Davids	1.13 pm

b) Rachel arrives in Taunton at 11.55 am. How long does she have to wait for the train to Exeter St Davids? $\boxed{}$

Activity | Find a train or bus timetable at home. Pick **two** places and try to work out the **length of time** between each stop.

Learning Objective:

"I can use am and pm, and work out time intervals."

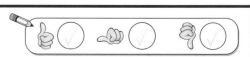

SHEET 3   © 2008 CGP

Time

1 Joe gets a digital watch for his birthday which uses a 24 hour clock. He gets home from school at a quarter to five. Write how his new watch displays this time.

a) [   ]

b) He eats his tea an hour and a half later.
    How does his watch display this time? [   ]

2 Write these 24 hour clock times using a 12 hour clock and am or pm.

a) (23:50)   b) (17:31)   c) (0:11)

[:   ]   [:   ]   [:   ]

3 Look at the swimming pool timetable.

a) Write the start and finish times for the
    sessions when the pool is open to the public.

    [   ]

b) For how long is the pool open to the public on Monday?

    [   ]

c) Dan is catching the bus to play canoe polo. It takes 27
    minutes. He catches it at 18.34. What time will he
    get to the swimming pool? Will he be early or late?

    [   ]

	Monday
7.00	
8.00	Open to the public
9.00	
10.00	School booking
11.00	
12.00	
13.00	
14.00	Open to the public
15.00	
16.00	
17.00	
18.00	Aquafit
19.00	Canoe polo
20.00	Lifesaving club
21.00	
22.00	

Activity Try setting a timer to record a TV programme or a film at home in the evening. What time will you need to <u>start</u> the timer? How <u>long</u> will it record for and when will it <u>finish</u>?

Learning Objective:

"I can use a 24 hour clock."

          © 2008 CGP

Time

1 | Jim looks at the calendar to see that it's the 23ʳᵈ August. He knows he's missed his mum's birthday by a week, and that it's his dad's birthday in a week.

August						
S	M	T	W	T	F	S
					1	2
3	4	5	6	7	8	9
10	11	12	13	14	15	16
17	18	19	20	21	22	23
24	25	26	27	28	29	30
31						

a) What is the date of his mum's birthday?

b) What is the date of his dad's birthday?

c) Jim's mum and dad were born in the same year. How many days older is his mum?

2 | Anita's birthday is on August 11ᵗʰ. She has a party on the Saturday before her birthday.

a) On what day of the week is her birthday?

b) What is the date of her party?

c) Her uncle can only come and see her on the Thursday after her birthday. What date is this?

3 | Dave has an appointment with the dentist on September 15ᵗʰ.

Open wide...

a) What day of the week is his appointment on?

b) The appointment gets cancelled and they offer him a new appointment which is 4 days later. What day is this on?

Activity | Using a calendar at home, try to work out the <u>number of days</u> between your family's birthdays, and the <u>days of the week</u> they fall on.

Learning Objective:

"I can use a calendar to work out dates and days of the week."

© 2008 CGP

Key Objective

Units and Measures

1 Write three and a half kilometres using these different units.

metres [ ]   centimetres [ ]

2 Circle the correct amount to complete the sentences.

a) Cardiff to London is about: 240 cm   240 m   240 km

b) An apple is likely to have a mass of about: 14 g   140 g   1400 g

c) The capacity of a saucepan is likely to be about: 2.5 ml   25 ml   2.5 l

d) The height of a room is likely to be about: 250 mm   250 cm   250 m

3 Write these distances in order from smallest to largest.

2 m   250 cm   20 cm   200 m   2 km   2.6 m

[ ]   [ ]   [ ]   [ ]   [ ]   [ ]

4 Estimate the length of the lines below.

Check your estimate by measuring the lines and writing the answer to the nearest half centimetre.

a) ───────────────   Estimate [ ]   Length [ ]

b) ──────────────────────   Estimate [ ]   Length [ ]

Activity Find some pencils and estimate their lengths in centimetres. Then check your estimates by measuring the pencils. Round your answers to the nearest half centimetre.

Learning Objective:

"I can estimate and measure a length using metres, centimetres or millimetres."

© 2008 CGP

Units and Measures

1 | **Estimate the length of the vulture's perch in cm.**

cm

Check your estimate by measuring
the perch to the nearest centimetre.

cm

2 | **One alien has a mass of 125 g. What is the mass of 6 aliens?**

Tick the scale which shows the correct reading.

3 | **Joanne has 2 vases.**

The first vase is full and contains 2.8 litres of water.
The second vase is half the capacity of the first and is half filled with water.

How much water does the second vase contain in ml?

Activity   Find a bag with lots of the same item in, such as a bag of apples, and
measure the mass of one of them. Count the items in the bag and
estimate the mass of the contents of the whole bag. Then measure the
mass of the whole bag. How close was your estimate to the real mass?

Learning Objective:

"I can estimate and measure length, mass and capacity."

© 2008 CGP

Units and Measures

1 | Mel buys a packet of fishfingers at the supermarket. |

The packet has a mass of 800 g and contains 40 fishfingers.

a) How much is 800 g in kilograms?

b) How many grams less than 1 kilogram is the packet of fishfingers?

c) What is the mass of one fishfinger?

2 | Convert the kilogram masses to grams. |

a) 3.6 kg

b) 4.5 kg

c) 9.9 kg

3 | Min goes running after school. She records how far she runs each day. |

Day 1	1700 m
Day 2	3.8 km
Day 3	4.3 km

a) Which day did she run the furthest?

b) How many metres did she run in total on the three days?

| Activity | Find out how far it is in km from your home to the nearest airport. Then convert the distance to metres and then centimetres. |

Learning Objective:

"I can convert larger to smaller units."

© 2008 CGP

Key Objective

Units and Measures

1   Bob buys some water bombs.

The water bombs each hold 150 ml of water.

a)   Bob used 1050 ml of water to fill some water bombs.
How many did he fill?

b)   How many litres of water would be needed for 100 water bombs?

2   Convert these amounts:

a)   2310 ml to l.

b)   6.74 kg to g.

c)   15.5 m to cm.

d)   1250 m to km.

3   Fido's lead is 6 metres long. The perimeter of his kennel is 120 cm.

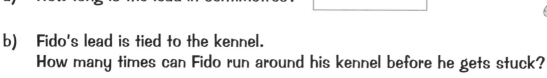

a)   How long is the lead in centimetres?

b)   Fido's lead is tied to the kennel.
How many times can Fido run around his kennel before he gets stuck?

c)   How many meters long would the lead need to be so that Fido could run
8 times around his kennel?

Activity   How many millilitres does your favourite mug hold?
Convert this into litres.

Learning Objective:

"I can convert from one unit of measure to another."

© 2008 CGP

Analysing Data

1 | Find the mode of each set of numbers. | The mode is the most common.

a) 2, 3, 4, 4, 5, 5, 6, 6, 6, 7, 8, 8   The mode is ☐

b) 9, 9, 8, 8, 8, 7, 6, 5, 5, 5, 5, 2   The mode is ☐

c) 2, 4, 5, 2, 6, 7, 7, 2, 3, 4, 2, 2   The mode is ☐

2 | Jamie has a collection of old coins. He sorts his coins by type.

The table shows how many of each coin he has.

farthing	halfpenny	penny	sixpence	shilling
48	67	134	121	15

a)   What is the mode type of coin?

b)   How many old coins does Jamie have altogether?

3 | Jamie then decides to sort his coins by age.

The table shows how many coins he has in each age range.

before 1850	1850-1875	1876-1900	1901-1925	after 1925
2	18	54	261	50

What is the mode age range of his coins?

Activity   Use a box of Lego® bricks or something similar for this activity.
Sort the pieces by colour and sort them by size.
Record your results in frequency tables.
What is the mode colour? What is the mode size?

Learning Objective:

"I can find the mode of a set of data."

© 2008 CGP

Analysing Data

1  **What is the mode of this set of numbers?**

13, 4, 28, 7, 4, 13, 4, 28   The mode is ▢

2 **Write a number in each box so that the mode of the numbers is 9.**

▢ ▢ ▢ ▢ ▢ ▢ ▢

3 **Alicia counted the insects in her garden.**

Alicia counted <u>54</u> insects altogether.
She sorted them into categories like this:

Ants   20
Beetles   12
Ladybirds 5
Flies   14
Bees

a) Alicia's page has torn.
    Work out how many bees she saw in her garden.

b) What was the mode type of insect she saw?

4 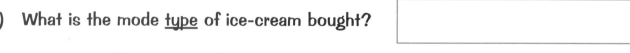 **Mrs Peterson bought ice-creams for everyone on a school trip.**

She wrote down what she bought and how much each ice-cream cost.

Type of ice-cream	sombrero	twisty	ninety-eight	magnet
Cost each	£1.20	£0.80	£1.00	£1.20
Number bought	20	5	24	16

a) What is the mode <u>cost</u> of an ice-cream?   £ ▢

b) What is the mode <u>type</u> of ice-cream bought?   ▢

Activity   Look at a page of a book or newspaper. Count the number of words on each line and the number of letters in each word. Record your results in frequency tables. What is the mode number of words on a line? What is the mode number of letters in a word?

Learning Objective:

"I can find the mode of a set of data."

   © 2008 CGP

Analysing Data

1 | **Seven friends are going on holiday together.**

The table shows how much spending money each friend takes.

Sam	Ed	Kate	Jane	Joe	Sarah	Tim
£20	£50	£20	£40	£60	£70	£20

a)   What is the total amount of spending money they have between them?

b)   What is the mean amount of spending money?

c)   What is the range of spending money?

2 | **The friends wanted to go on a day trip. They had these options:**

Boat trip	Balloon ride	Walk	Tour of city	Museum
2 hours	1 hour	5 hours	3 hours	1 hour

a)   What is the mode length of time for a trip?

b)   What is the median length of time for a trip?

3 | **Find the mean, median and range of this set of numbers.**

8.2, 4.7, 2.8, 7.2, 1.4, 12.8, 4.2

Mean:

Median:

Range:

Activity

Shuffle an ordinary pack of playing cards. Take the top four cards and add together their values (all face cards are worth ten). Repeat this for each set of four cards through the pack. Write down your score each time. Find the mean, median and range of your scores.

Learning Objective:

"I can solve problems using mode, range, median and mean."

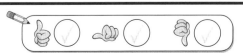

SHEET 3

© 2008 CGP

<u>Chance and Likelihood</u>

1 | **Choose a word from the box to describe each of these events:**

You may use each word once, more than once or not at all.

certain   likely   unlikely   impossible

a)   It will snow in the winter.

b)   You roll a normal dice and score 6 or less.

c)   It will not rain in England for two months.

d)   You will have ice-cream for breakfast.

e)   You flap your arms and find you can fly.

2 | **This spinner has six equal sections.**

Shade the spinner so there is an equal chance
of landing on a shaded or an unshaded part.

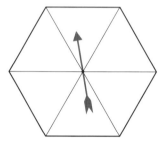

3 | **Adam rolls a normal dice with the faces numbered 1 to 6.**

For each pair of outcomes below, underline the one that is more likely.
If the outcomes are equally likely, underline both of them.

He rolls a **one.** | OR | He rolls a **six.**

He rolls an **odd number.** | OR | He rolls an **even number.**

He rolls a **multiple of two.** | OR | He rolls a **multiple of three.**

| **Activity** | Think of your own events that are <u>certain</u> and <u>impossible</u>.
Write down as many of each as you can.

<u>Learning Objective:</u>

"I can describe how likely it is that an event will happen
and justify my statement."

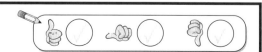

© 2008 CGP

Chance and Likelihood

1 | Lilly has a bag of 16 marbles. |

Some are <u>black</u>, some are <u>white</u>,
some are <u>spotty</u> and some are <u>striped</u>.

She shakes the bag, then takes out
a marble without looking.

a) Which type of marble is she most likely to take out?

b) Which 2 types of marble does she have an equal chance of taking out?

| | and | |

c) Is she more likely to take out a striped or a spotty one?

2 | This spinner has 10 equal sections. |

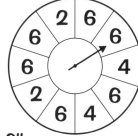

Ryan spins the spinner.

a) Which 2 numbers have an equal chance of coming up?

| | and | |

b) Ryan says, "I have a greater than even chance of landing on 6".
Is he correct?

Circle Yes or No.

Explain your answer.

3 | Mark the letter of each event on the line where you think it belongs. |

| Impossible | Unlikely | Even Chance | Likely | Certain |

A: A new baby will be a girl   C: I will have a drink today
B: It will be frosty in January   D: The next book I read will have exactly 248 pages

| Activity | Pick a card from an ordinary deck of playing cards.
Describe the likelihood of: a) it being a queen. b) it being a red card.
Make up some more outcomes and describe the chance of each one.

Learning Objective:

"I can describe how likely it is that an event will happen
and justify my statement."

SHEET **2**

© 2008 CGP

Chance and Likelihood

1 | This spinner has 8 equal sections. |

Draw more shapes on the spinner so that all three sentences in the box are true.

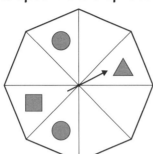

> It is certain that you will spin a triangle, a circle or a square.
>
> You have an equal chance of spinning a circle or a triangle.
>
> You are least likely to spin a square.

2 | Estimate the chance of each of these events happening. Mark each letter on the line where you think it belongs. |

The first one has been done for you.

Impossible   Even Chance   Certain

A It will rain in April.
B You will play sport in the next week.
C You win a game of snakes and ladders against your friend.
D You will drive yourself to school tomorrow.
E You pick a face card from a standard pack of playing cards.

3 | Here are two spinners, A and B. |

Circle true or false under each statement:

a) Scoring a **3** is more likely on **A** than **B**.
      TRUE / FALSE

b) Scoring a **5** is more likely on **A** than **B**.
      TRUE / FALSE

c) Scoring a **4** is equally likely on **A** and **B**.
      TRUE / FALSE

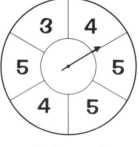

Spinner A

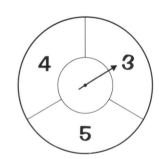
Spinner B

| Activity | Imagine spinning both spinners from question **3** and adding the scores together. What scores are possible? What is the most likely score? What is the least likely one? Try it with some different spinners.

Learning Objective:

"I can use the language of chance to solve problems."

© 2008 CGP

Conclusions

1 | The bar charts show the favourite colours of boys and girls in Year 6. |

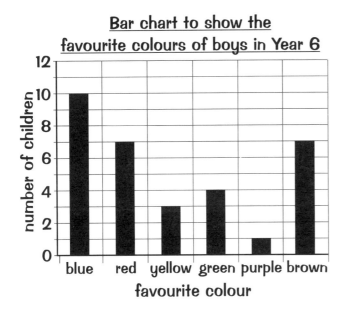

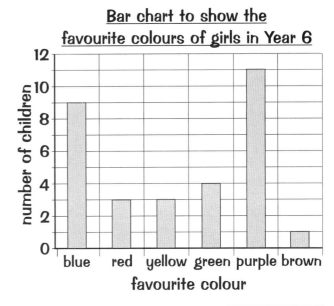

a) How many people in total chose yellow as their favourite colour? ☐

b) Which colours were equally popular with boys and girls?

☐ and ☐

c) Kate says "blue is not a girl's colour".
Explain how the chart shows that she is wrong.

d) Write a question of your own that can be answered using the bar charts.

Activity | Carry out your own survey. Ask friends and family to choose their favourite colour from the 6 given above. Comment on your results. Does the choice of colour depend on gender? Or age?

Learning Objective:

"I can explain what a table, graph or chart tells us and consider questions that it raises."

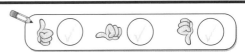

© 2008 CGP

Conclusions

1 | Jonathan went for a bike ride. The table shows his distance from where he started at various points along the way.

Time (minutes)	0	10	20	30	40	50	60	70	80	90	100	110	120
Distance (km)	0	4	8	12	16	16	11	4	4	3	2	1	0

a) Complete this line graph of his ride.

If you have access to a computer, you could draw the graph using Microsoft® Excel® instead. Print your graph and stick it to your worksheet.

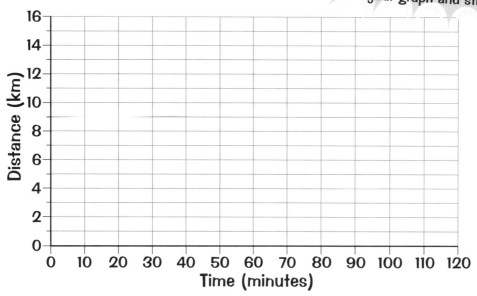

b) How long did it take Jonathan to travel 12 km? [   ] minutes

c) What might Jonathan have been doing between 40 and 50 minutes and between 70 and 80 minutes?

d) Write a question of your own that can be answered using the line graph.

| Activity | Find a table, graph or chart in a newspaper or magazine. Write down at least three questions you could answer from the data.

Learning Objective:

"I can explain what a table, graph or chart tells us and consider questions that it raises."

© 2008 CGP

Conclusions

1 | **In the UK temperatures are measured in degrees Celsius (°C). In America, they are measured in degrees Fahrenheit (°F).**

The graph shows how to convert degrees Celsius into degrees Fahrenheit.

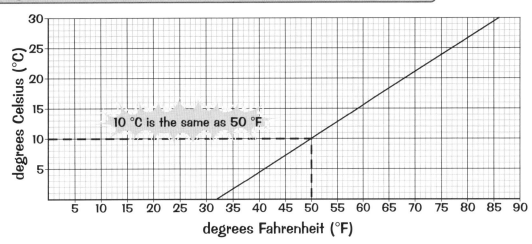

10 °C is the same as 50 °F

The table shows average temperatures from New York (in °F) and Manchester (in °C):

	January	February	March	April	May	June	July	August	September	October	November	December
New York (in °F)	32	30	41	51	62	69	75	77	64	52	35	28
Manchester (in °C)	0	4	5	7	10	15	17	22	16	9	6	3

a) What was the hottest average temperature in New York? Give your answer in °F and then in °C.   [ ] °F   [ ] °C

b) What was the coolest average temperature in Manchester? Give your answer in °C and then in °F.   [ ] °C   [ ] °F

c) What was the difference in temperature between the two cities in March? Give your answer in °C.

d) Evie says "It's always warmer in New York than Manchester". Is she correct? Circle Yes or No. Explain your answer.

Activity   Find out the daily temperature where you live over a week. You could watch the weather on TV or look on the internet. Make a line graph and comment on your findings. Was it hotter or colder at the start of the week? Why?

Learning Objective:

"I can use data to solve problems."

© 2008 CGP

Key
Objective

Data

1 | You are helping to plan a party for a Year 2 class. |

You need to decide:
- How to decorate the hall.
- What games to play.
- What food and drink to have at the party.

You will need a questionnaire to find out what the children would like.

a) You decide to decorate the hall with balloons.
Write a question to help you choose what colours to use.

b) Think of five different games you could play at the party.
Draw a table that you could use to find the most popular games.

c) Write three questions to help you decide what food and drink to have.
In your questions, give options to choose from.

| Activity | Answer this question: "Which word comes up most on a page of my reading book?" Count the common words "a", "the", "in", "is", "to" and "of". Make a tally chart. |

Learning Objective:

"I can decide what data I need to collect and put it into a table to help me answer questions."

© 2008 CGP

Data

1 | Jane works in a shop that sells school clothes by age. |

She recorded the sizes of all the pairs of trousers she sold over a week.

	Trousers sold by size					
Monday	9	9	11	13		
Tuesday	12	8	10	13		
Wednesday	8	11	10	10	10	
Thursday	9	8	8	8	14	
Friday	9	9	13	8	10	
Saturday	14	14	14	9	12	8

a) Fill in this frequency table to show how many pairs of trousers of each size she sold over the week.

Size						
Tally						
Frequency						

b) Which size of trousers did Jane sell the most of?

2 | You want to answer this question: |

"What is the most common colour of car in your area?"

Describe how you would collect information to answer this question.
Think about <u>where</u> and <u>for how long</u> you would collect the data.

Activity
You will need an ordinary 6-sided dice. Roll the dice 50 times.
Record your score on each roll in a frequency table.
Do you notice any numbers coming up more than others?

Learning Objective:

"I can decide what information needs to be collected to answer a question and how best to collect it."

© 2008 CGP

Key Objective

Data

1 **Isaac's class had these questions to answer:**

1. How much television do children in our class watch each week?

2. Do children in our class watch more television on some days than other days?

a) Describe what Isaac's class could do to collect data to answer these questions.

The table shows the total number of hours of television watched by each child in Isaac's class over 1 week. The times are recorded to the nearest half an hour.

6	12	8.5	13.5	9	9.5	14	9	15	7
15.5	7.5	8.5	3	11	12.5	8	15.5	7.5	16
12.5	11	10.5	9	4.5	15	11	6	10	7.5

b) Complete this table from the data:

Hours watched	0 to 3	3.5 to 6	6.5 to 9	9.5 to 12	12.5 to 15	15.5 to 18
Tally						
Frequency						

c) What was the most common amount of time children spent watching TV?   ☐ to ☐ hours

d) What could Isaac's class do to answer the question:
"Do children in our class watch more television on some days than others?"

Activity Find out about the type of television programme your friends and family like to watch. Make a frequency table and pie chart from your data.

Learning Objective:

"I can collect data in a variety of ways and use my results to solve problems."

© 2008 CGP

Key Objective

Tables and Charts

1 Jo counted how many books were borrowed from the library each hour.

Time	Tally	Total
9 am - 10 am	IIII IIII IIII II	17
10 am - 11 am	IIII III	8
11 am - 12 noon		2
12 noon - 1 pm	IIII IIII IIII IIII III	
1 pm - 2 pm		14
2 pm - 3 pm	IIII IIII IIII	
3 pm - 4 pm		5

a) Complete this frequency table.

b) How many books were borrowed between 9 am and 11 am?

c) Were more books borrowed in the morning or the afternoon?

d) On a sheet of squared paper, draw a pictogram of this information.

Use:
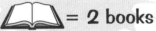 = 2 books

2 These bar charts show how many books Kim read each month this year.

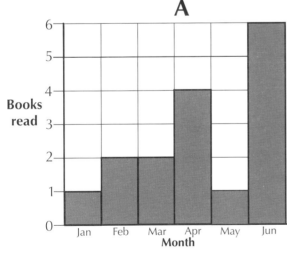

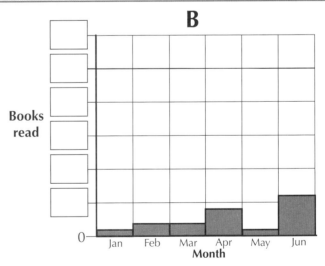

a) Complete the missing numbers on the scale of bar chart **B**.

b) Which bar chart makes it look like Kim reads lots of books?

Activity Deal 30 cards from a shuffled pack.
Draw a frequency table to show how many you dealt of each suit.

Learning Objective:

"I can use tables, tally charts, pictograms and bar charts."

Key Objective

Tables and Charts

1 Kath's Cafe sells coffees, cakes and cookies.
The chart shows how many of each were sold on Wednesday.

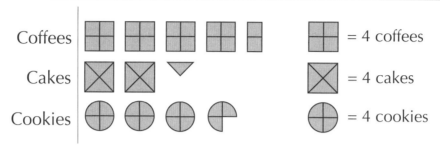

Coffees	= 4 coffees
Cakes	= 4 cakes
Cookies	= 4 cookies

a) The cafe had 16 slices of cake at the beginning of the day.
How many slices did the cafe have left at the end of the day?

b) On Thursday the cafe sold twice as many coffees as on Wednesday.
How many coffees did the cafe sell on Thursday?

c) On some squared paper, draw a bar chart
to show what the cafe sold on Wednesday.

2 This chart shows how many people went
to a hairdresser each day one week.

✂ = 5 people

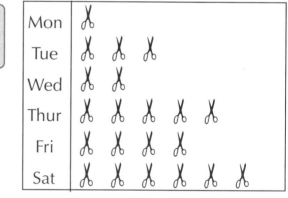

a) How many more people went to the
hairdresser on Thursday than on Tuesday?

b) How many people went to the hairdresser in total that week?

c) On a separate piece of paper make a frequency table of this data.

Activity Count how many cups, plates, bowls and pans are in
your kitchen cupboards at home.
Make a frequency table and a pictogram of this data.
Think of three questions that you could use your pictogram to answer.

Learning Objective:

"I can make and understand pictograms, bar charts and
frequency tables."

© 2008 CGP

Tables and Charts

Key
Objective

1 The graph shows the distance travelled every 15 minutes when Year 6 went on a coach trip.

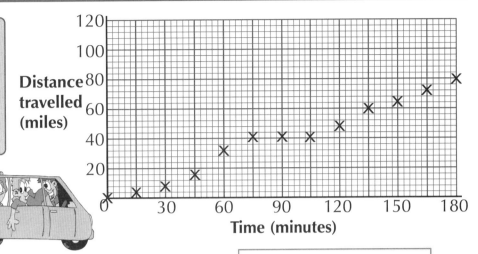

Distance travelled (miles) vs Time (minutes)

a) How far had they travelled after 45 minutes? [   ] miles

b) At one point the coach stopped for half an hour. How many miles from school was this? [   ] miles

2 Year 6 did a sponsored silence. The table shows how long it was before children spoke, to the nearest minute.

Minutes before speaking	Number of children
6-10 minutes	5
11-15 minutes	8
16-20 minutes	27
21-25 minutes	21
26-30 minutes	14

a) On some squared paper, make a bar chart of this data.

b) How many children were silent for more than 20 minutes? [   ]

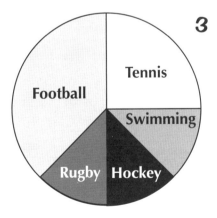

3 The pie chart shows the favourite sports of a class of 24 children.

a) What fraction of the class like tennis best? [   ]

b) How many children like swimming best? [   ]

c) What fraction of the class prefer football? [   ]

Activity Throw two dice 30 times. Add up the total shown on both dice each time. Make a frequency table to show how many times you threw 2-5, 6-8, and 9-12. Draw a bar chart of your results.

Learning Objective:

"I can represent data in a variety of ways and answer questions about the data, including interpreting pie charts."

© 2008 CGP

Answers

Page 1 — Explaining Problem Solving, Sheet 3

Q1 a) $18 \div 3 = 6$
b) $24 - 9 = 15$
c) $42 + 12 = 54$

Q2 $£4.30 + £2.45 = £6.75$

Q3 **Offer 1** is cheaper.
Offer 1 costs 40p, but offer 2 costs 45p.

Activity:
Many possible answers. For example:
Stavros the cheetah catches four mice every day. How many does he catch in a week?
There are 7 days in a week, so the answer is $4 \times 7 = 28$.

Page 2 — Explaining Problem Solving, Sheet 4

Q1 a) Rosie is most likely to pull out a **mint chocolate**. There are 4 mint chocolates, but only 2 orange chocolates and 1 plain chocolate.
b) Rosie is now most likely to pull out an **orange chocolate**. There are five orange chocolates altogether, but only 4 mint chocolates and 1 plain chocolate.

Q2 A square number is found by multiplying another number by itself. $25 = 5 \times 5$, so 25 is a square number.
Possible diagram:

$5 \times 5 = 25$

Q3 The perimeter is **48 m**.

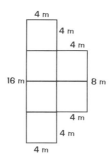

$4 \, m + 4 \, m + 4 \, m + 8 \, m$
$+ 4 \, m + 4 \, m + 4 \, m + 16 \, m$
$= 48 \, m$

Activity:
The number combinations are:

Score	Combinations
3	2 + 1
5	1 + 4, 2 + 3
6	1 + 5, 2 + 4, 3 + 3
8	2 + 6, 3 + 5, 4 + 4
10	4 + 6, 5 + 5
11	5 + 6
12	6 + 6

Page 3 — Explaining Problem Solving, Sheet 5

Q1 The number is **42**.
$7 \times 6 = 42$, so
42 is a multiple of 7.
42 ends in 2.
$4 + 2 = 6$, so the sums of its digits is 6.

Q2 a) ▢ = 4
▲ = 3
● = 5

b) The **triangle** is the first shape value to work out. There are 4 triangles in a row. They add up to 12.
So ▲ $= 12 \div 4 = 3$

Activity:
They bought **4 small popcorns** and **2 large popcorns**.

2 large popcorns cost
$2 \times £1.60 = £3.20$.
This leaves
$£8.00 - £3.20 = £4.80$
to spend on small popcorns.
Now $£4.80 = 4 \times £1.20$.
So they can buy exactly 4 small popcorns.

Page 4 — Explaining Problem Solving, Sheet 6

Q1 a)

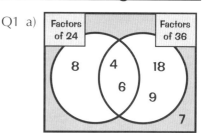

b) Factors come in pairs — for example 4×9. If the factors in each pair are different, they will always add up to give an even number of factors.
36 is a square number, so one of the factors multiplies by itself (6×6). So 36 has an even number of distinct factors, and 6 on its own. This gives an odd number of factors altogether.

Q2

	Curry	Pasta	Total
Year 5	26	21	47
Year 6	23	19	42
Total	49	40	89

Answers

Q3   A cheeseburger costs **£1.50**
A hotdog costs **£1.20**
A portion of chips costs **80p**

2 cheeseburgers and 1 portion of chips costs £3.80.
1 cheeseburger and 1 portion of chips costs £2.30.
So 1 cheeseburger costs £3.80 – £2.30 = £1.50.
Now
1 cheeseburger and 1 portion of chips costs £2.30.
So 1 portion of chips costs £2.30 – £1.50 = £0.80 = 80p.
Finally
1 hotdog and 1 portion of chips costs £2.00.
So 1 hotdog costs £2.00 – £0.80 = £1.20

Activity:
There are **6 ways** that Scarlett's friends can sit.
S = Scarlett, A = Adam,
D = Davina, G = Greg

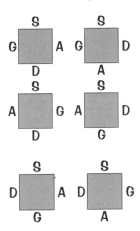

Page 5 — Explaining Problem Solving, Sheet 7

Q1   Ellie's number was **66**.
You could have used the inverse to work out your answer:
? ÷ 2 × 10 = 330
Now 330 ÷ 10 = 33
So ? = 33 × 2 = 66.

Q2   **Asid is correct.** There are 5 even numbers on the spinner but only three odd numbers. This means there is a greater chance of an even number coming up.

Q3 a)   **Lauren is correct** because the 1st negative number in the sequence will be –8. The sequence goes down in steps of 10, so every negative number in the sequence will end in 8.

    b)   The first negative number in the sequence below –100 will be **–108**. This is the first number less than –100 that ends in 8.

Activity:
6 different amounts could be made:
30p (10p + 20p)
12p (10p + 2p)
15p (10p + 5p)
22p (20p + 2p)
25p (20p + 5p)
7p (2p + 5p)

Page 6 — Number Patterns, Sheet 4

Q1 a)   32, 36, 40, **44**, **48**, 52 — rule is **add 4**.

    b)   450, 400, 350, **300**, **250**, **200** — rule is **subtract 50**.

    c)   0, 20, 40, 60, **80**, **100**, 120 — rule is **add 20**.

Q2   Any of the following are correct for a) and b):
23 + 74
34 + 27
43 + 72
32 + 47

    c)   **odd + even** or **even + odd**

Q3

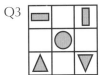

Activity:
3p (2p + 1p), 4p (2p + 2p),
6p (5p + 1p), 7p (5p + 2p),
11p (10p + 1p), 12p (10p + 2p),
15p (10p + 5p).

Page 7 — Number Patterns, Sheet 5

Q1 a)   63, 51, **39**, 27, 15, 3 — rule is **subtract 12**.

    b)   80, 105, **130**, **155**, **180**, 205 — rule is **add 25**.

    c)   3, 6, 12, 24, 48, 96 — rule is **double the previous number**.

Q2   **Yes, Jane is correct. If you can divide the last 2 digits of a number by 4, you can divide the whole number by 4 and
28 ÷ 4 = 7.**

Q3   My number was **12**. You can prove this by reversing the calculation:
31 – 7 = 24
24 ÷ 2 = 12

Q4 a)   **False**
True

    b)   **Possible answers: Shape A has 2 right angles, Shape A has 2 acute angles (angles less than 90º), Shape A has 2 reflex angles (angles greater than 180º)**

    c)   **Possible answer: Shape B has 2 lines of symmetry.**

Activity:
3, 9, 15, 21, 27, 33, 39, 45

Page 8 — Number Patterns, Sheet 6

Q1 a)   13, 19, 25, **31**, **37**, **43**, 49 — rule is **add 6**.

    b)   2, 0, –2, **–4**, **–6**, **–8**, **–10** — rule is **subtract 2**.

    c)   480, 240, **120**, 60, 30, 15 — rule is **divide the previous answer by 2**.

    d)   7, 10, 17, **27**, 44, 71, 115 — rule is **add the 2 previous numbers**.

Answers

Q2 a) **72 chocolate bars**

b) **10 boxes**

c) **Number of boxes × 15 = Number of chocolate bars**

Q3 a) 4

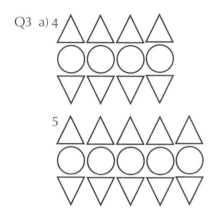

b) **200 triangles. The rule is: Number of triangles = Shape number × 2.**

Activity

 = 5   = 20

Page 9 — Planning Problem Solving, Sheet 4

Q1

	Only straight lines	Only curved lines	Straight and curved lines
No lines of symmetry	N	S	G
One or more lines of symmetry	A	C	D

Q2 a) **11** should be written in the table (shown below).

b) 11 + 1 = **12**

c) 7 + 11 + 12 = 30
32 − 30 = **2**

Type of newt	Tally	Total
Smooth	JHT II	7
Palmate	JHT JHT I	11
Crested	JHT JHT II	12
Banded	II	2

Q3 a) 5 cherry buns cost 5 × 15p = 75p.
If Charlotte buys 5 cherry buns, she'll have 200p (£2) − 75p = 125p.
5 iced buns cost 5 × 25p = 125p.
So Charlotte **can** afford to buy 5 cherry buns and 5 iced buns.

b) 4 cream buns cost 4 × 20p = 80p.
4 cherry buns = 4 × 15p = 60p.
2 iced buns = 2 × 25p = 50p.
Total = 80p + 60p + 50p = 190p.
200p − 190p = 10p.
Charlotte's change from £2 is **10p.**

Activity:
Many possible answers, e.g. "In my name / Not in my name", "Vowel / Consonant", "Has a gap in it / Is a closed shape", etc.

Page 10 — Planning Problem Solving, Sheet 5

Q1 a)

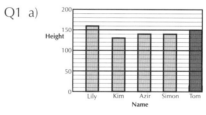

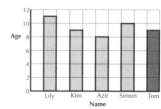

b)

	Shorter than 150 cm	150 cm or taller
10 or older	Simon	Lily
Younger than 10	Azir Kim	Tom

Q2 a) **Amy**

b) **Charlie**

c) Many possible answers, e.g. "Who owns a cat but not a fish?" (Ella), "How many children own a rabbit?" (1), etc.

Activity:
There are **eight** different possibilities:
Vanilla ice cream, chocolate sauce, marshmallows.
Vanilla ice cream, chocolate sauce, jelly beans.
Vanilla ice cream, toffee sauce, marshmallows.
Vanilla ice cream, toffee sauce, jelly beans.
Strawberry ice cream, chocolate sauce, marshmallows.
Strawberry ice cream, chocolate sauce, jelly beans.
Strawberry ice cream, toffee sauce, marshmallows.
Strawberry ice cream, toffee sauce, jelly beans.

Page 11 — Planning Problem Solving, Sheet 6

Q1 a) Possible answers are **724, 729, 741** and **742.**

b) Many possible answers, e.g. "Make a 2-digit even number greater than 24 but less than 94 using the cards" (e.g. 42, 72, 74, 92).

Q2 a) **Class 2** (14 boys + 12 girls = 26 children).

b) **Class 5** (Class 3 has 31 children, Class 5 has 33).

c) Many possible answers, e.g. "Which class has the most girls?" (Class 4), "Which two classes have more girls than boys?" (Class 1 and Class 4).

Q3 a) You can buy a pineapple, a bag of apples and a cauliflower for less than £3 — **true** (£1.05 + 98p + 95p = £2.98).

Answers

It costs more to buy bananas and carrots than to buy broccoli and tomatoes — **false** (bananas and carrots = 82p + 31p = £1.13, broccoli and tomatoes = 67p + 69p = £1.36).

If you pay for 2 cauliflowers and a bag of apples with £3, you get 17p change — **false**, you get 12p change (£3.00 − £2.88 = 12p).

b) Many possible answers, e.g. "use a bigger selection of fruit and vegetables — pears, potatoes, strawberries, etc".

Activity:
a) **36** (6 × 6).
b) **1**, **2**, **3**, **4**, **5**, **6**, **8, 9** and **10**.
c) Many possible answers, e.g. "How many even numbers can you make?" (12 — 2, 4, 6, 8, 10, 12, 16, 18, 20, 24, 30, 36).

Page 12 — Problem Solving, Sheet 5

Q1   215.3 − 87.4 = **127.9** m

Q2 a) 39 + 31 + 23 + 16 = **109**
   b) 31 − 14 = **17**
   c) 23 + 16 = **39**

Q3   Shop A: £179.99 + £39.99
              = £219.98

       Shop B: £189.95 + £36.50
              = £226.45

       Difference: £226.45 −
       £219.98
                   = **£6.47**

Activity:
E.g. If petrol costs £1.16 per litre, and it costs £40 to fill up the tank, then 40 ÷ 1.16 = about 34 litres.

Page 13 — Problem Solving, Sheet 6

Q1   1.5 ÷ 12 = **0.125 l** or **125 ml**

Q2 a) 6 ÷ 0.86 = 6.98
      = **6 loaves**
   b) 6 × £0.86 = £5.16.
      £6.00 − £5.16 = **£0.84** or **84p**

Q3 a) (0.42 × 1.5) + (0.39 × 1.5) + (0.87 × 1.5) = **£2.52**

   b) (0.42 × 2) + (0.87 × 3) + (0.39 × 2) = £4.23.
      £4.23 ÷ 10 = **£0.42**

Activity:
E.g. 2.6 kg of apples would cost 2.6 × 0.29 = **£0.75**.

Page 14 — Problem Solving, Sheet 7

Q1   14.6 + 14.6 + 3.8 + 3.8 = **36.8 m**

Q2   2.35 + 5.99 = 2.35 + 6 − 0.01 = 8.34
       20 − 8.34 = 12 − 0.34 = **£11.66**

Q3 a) 2000 ÷ 20 = **100**
   b) 100 × 185 = **18500 ml** or **18.5 l**

Q4   £12 ÷ 10 = **£1.20**

Activity:
Find the sum of the price of 5 books.
E.g. £5.99 + £6.49 + £9.99 + £4.79 + £6.99 = **£34.25**

Page 15 — Problem Solving, Sheet 8

Q1 a) 0.2 × 16.50 = 3.30.
      16.50 + 3.30 = **£19.80**
   b) 0.2 × 11.20 = 2.24
      11.20 + 2.24 = **£13.44**
   c) 0.2 × 1.25 = 0.25
      1.25 + 0.25 = **£1.50**

Q2 a) 60 ÷ 8 = 7.5.
      7.5 × 4 = **30 cm**
   b) length = 22.5, height = 7.5.
      Area = 22.5 × 7.5 = **168.75 cm²**

Q3   £20 − £14.02 = £5.98.
      £5.98 ÷ 2 = **£2.99**

Activity:

	sesame seeds	peanuts	maize	oatmeal
500 g	125 g	50 g	150 g	175 g
1 kg	250 g	100 g	300 g	350 g
5 kg	1250 g	500 g	1500 g	1750 g

Page 16 — Write and Draw to Solve Problems, Sheet 3

Q1 a)

   b) **12**

Q2 a) **12 − 5**
   b) **22 − 5**

Q3 a) **50p**
   b) **75p**
   c) 7 × 25p (= 175p or £1.75)
      or 25p + 25p + 25p + 25p + 25p + 25p + 25p (= 175p or £1.75)

Activity:
You need 2 more matchsticks/pens and pencils each time.

Page 17 — Write and Draw to Solve Problems, Sheet 4

Q1   220 + 12 = 232 seats needed. 4 coaches have 212 seats, which is too few. 5 coaches have 265 seats, which is enough.
      They will need **5** coaches.

Q2 a)

Number of nights	1	2	3	4	5	6
Total cost	£35	£70	£105	£140	£175	£210

   b) 6 × £5 = **£30**
   c) Breakfast at hotel costs £45 − £35 = £10.
      This is £5 more expensive per day than cafe, so saving is 6 × £5 = **£30**.

Activity:
7 jumps are needed for 5 steps. And, e.g. 11 steps are needed for 7 steps.

Answers

Page 18 — Write and Draw to Solve Problems, Sheet 5

Q1 **16.90 – 3.75**

Q2 Any 3 combinations that add up to £38.50.
E.g. **(7 × £5) + (3 × £1) + (1 × 50p)**
(6 × £5) + (8 × £1) + (1 × 50p)
(6 × £5) + (5 × £1) + (7 × 50p)

Q3 a) 30 × £6.50 =
(30 × £6) + (30 × £0.50) =
£180 + £15 = **£195**
b) 30 × £2.70 =
(30 × £2) + (30 × £0.70) =
£60 + £21 = £81
£81 + £195 = **£276**

Activity:
7 triangles are possible:
6 cm, 5 cm, 4 cm
6 cm, 5 cm, 3 cm
6 cm, 5 cm, 2 cm
6 cm, 4 cm, 3 cm
5 cm, 4 cm, 3 cm
5 cm, 4 cm, 2 cm
4 cm, 3 cm, 2 cm
Record so that no triangles are repeated.

Page 19 — Write and Draw to Solve Problems, Sheet 6

Q1 **7 ×** ▲

Q2 12 + 12 = ▲ + ▲ + 12
12 = ▲ + ▲
So ▲ = **6**

Q3 a)

Minutes	Words
5	225
10	450
15	675
20	900
30	1350
60	2700

b) Find the time that is nearest to 1000 words. Add or subtract 1 minute's worth of words until the answer is as close to 1000 words as possible.

Activity:
Multiply the cost of a drink and ice cream by the number of people in the family.

Page 20 — Counting and Sequences, Sheet 3

Q1 a) **64, 68, 72**
b) **800, 825, 850**

Q2 a) **81, 91, 101**
b) **0, 30, 60**

Q3 a)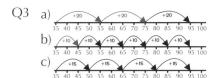
b)
c)

Activity:
Jumping along from 0 in steps of 2 means you always land on even numbers.
Steps of 3 mean you alternate between odd and even numbers.

Page 21 — Counting and Sequences, Sheet 4

Q1 a) **–7, –5, –3**
b) **–7, –4, ... 11**
c) **12, 12.6, 13.2**
d) **2.4, 2.1, 1.8**

Q2 15 °C, **12 °C, 9 °C, 6 °C, 3 °C, 0 °C, –3 °C**

Q3 **–20, –11**

Q4 0.6 kg, **1.2 kg, 1.8 kg, 2.4 kg, 3.0 kg**

Activity:
5.6, 4.2, 2.8, 1.4, 0
So, 4 times as tall.

Page 22 — Counting and Sequences, Sheet 5

Q1 a) **–38, –29, –20**
b) **25.6, 27.0, 28.4**
c) **0.1, 0.4, 0.7**
d) **–6.9, –5, –3.1**

Q2 a) **£4.25, £8.50, £12.75, £17.00, £21.25, £25.50**
b) **5**

Q3 a) **Add 4**
b) **Subtract 0.2**

Activity:
20, 19.1, 18.2, 17.3, 16.4, 15.5, 14.6, 13.7, 12.8, 11.9, 11.0, 10.1, 9.2, 8.3, 7.4, 6.5, 5.6, 4.7, 3.8, 2.9, 2.0, 1.1, 0.2
The units digits generally go down (there are blips around 11 and 2). The tenths digits go up.
The digits always sum to either 11 or 2.

Page 23 — Decimals, Sheet 2

Q1 **24**

Q2 **21p, £1.02, 120p, £1.21, £1.22**

Q3
Q4

Activity:
E.g. crisps 35p, pepper 69p, soup 99p, bread £1.08, jam £1.19, apples £1.36, potatoes £1.55, cake £1.99, box of chocolates £3.99, chicken £5.99.

Page 24 — Decimals, Sheet 3

Q1 a) **2.23 m, 2.19 m, 2.16 m, 2.05 m, 1.96 m, 1.85 m.**
b) **Rob**

Q2 a) 6.82 = **6 + 0.8 + 0.02**
b) 9.16 = **9 + 0.1 + 0.06**

Q3 a) **3 hundreds**
b) **2 thousands**
c) **4 units**
d) **8 tenths**
e) **5 hundredths**
f) **3 tens**

Activity:
Partition the price of 3 items on a shopping list. E.g. £3.49 = 3.0 + 0.4 + 0.09.

Answers

Page 25 — Decimals, Sheet 4

Q1

Q2 a) **1.412**
   b) **13.126**
   c) **0.556**

Q3 a) **4 units**
   b) **1 ten**
   c) **9 tenths**
   d) **0 hundredths**
   e) **8 thousandths**
   f) **6 hundreds**

Q4 a) **0.009**
   b) **0.07**

Activity:
E.g. 45.25 kg = 40 + 5 + 0.2 + 0.05

Page 26 — Fractions, Sheet 3

Q1

Q2

Q3 $1\frac{3}{4}$ $2\frac{1}{4}$ $2\frac{3}{10}$ $2\frac{4}{10}$ $3\frac{1}{2}$

Q4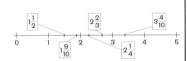

Activity:
E.g.

Page 27 — Fractions, Sheet 4

Q1 a) $\frac{5}{8}$

   b) $\frac{3}{8}$

Q2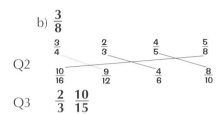

Q3 $\frac{2}{3}$ $\frac{10}{15}$

Q4 a) **6**
   b) **25**
   c) **20**
   d) **10**

Activity:
Find equivalent fractions by multiplying the numerator and denominator by the same number.

Page 28 — Fractions, Sheet 5

Q1 a) $\frac{3}{4}$

   b) $\frac{1}{2}$

   c) $\frac{2}{3}$

   d) $\frac{3}{7}$

   e) $\frac{2}{5}$

Q2 a) $\frac{6}{20}$ $\frac{10}{20}$ $\frac{12}{20}$ $\frac{15}{20}$ $\frac{16}{20}$

   b) $\frac{6}{20}$ $\frac{10}{20}$ $\frac{12}{20}$ $\frac{15}{20}$ $\frac{16}{20}$

Q3 a) $1\frac{1}{5}$

   b) $2\frac{4}{5}$

Activity:
E.g. $\frac{2}{6}$, $\frac{3}{9}$, $\frac{4}{12}$, $\frac{5}{15}$, $\frac{6}{18}$

Page 29 — Fractions and Decimals, Sheet 2

Q1 a) $\frac{4}{100}$ or $\frac{1}{25}$

   b) $\frac{75}{100}$ or $\frac{3}{4}$

   c) $\frac{6}{10}$ or $\frac{3}{5}$

   d) $\frac{25}{100}$ or $\frac{1}{4}$

Q2 $\frac{2}{10}$ = 0.2, $\frac{3}{4}$ = 0.75,
     $\frac{10}{100}$ = 0.1, $\frac{5}{100}$ = 0.05

Q3 a) $\frac{1}{4}$

   b) $\frac{2}{100}$

Q4 a) **0.6**
   b) **0.04**
   c) **0.75**
   d) **0.12**

Activity:
The 3rd decimal place is the thousandths place.
0.009 = $\frac{9}{1000}$, 0.023 = $\frac{23}{1000}$.

Page 30 — Fractions and Decimals, Sheet 3

Q1

$\frac{1}{2}$	$\frac{95}{100}$	$\frac{6}{10}$
$\frac{7}{10}$	$\frac{2}{10}$	$\frac{1}{4}$
$\frac{5}{20}$	$\frac{35}{100}$	$\frac{15}{100}$
$\frac{8}{10}$	$\frac{3}{4}$	$\frac{4}{10}$

0.5	0.95	0.6
0.7	0.2	0.25
0.25	0.35	0.15
0.8	0.75	0.4

Q2 a) Any **12 squares** shaded, e.g.

   b) Any **12 squares** shaded, e.g.

   c) Any **4 squares** shaded, e.g.

Q3 a) **0.5**
   b) **0.25**

148

Answers

Activity:
a) **0.23**
b) **0.30769...**
c) **0.7888...**
d) **0.308181...**

Page 31 — Fractions and Decimals, Sheet 4

Q1 a) **0.6, 0.9, 0.75, 0.4, 0.7**
b) **0.4, 0.6, 0.7, 0.75, 0.9**

Q2 **0.75, 0.2, 0.55, 0.4, 0.3**

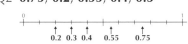

Q3 a) $\frac{2}{3}$ = **0.667 — largest**.
$\frac{5}{8}$ = **0.625**.
$\frac{6}{11}$ = **0.545**.
$\frac{8}{13}$ = **0.615**.
b) $\frac{3}{7}$ = **0.429**.
$\frac{11}{15}$ = **0.733 — largest**.
$\frac{9}{16}$ = **0.563**.
$\frac{4}{21}$ = **0.190**.

Activity:
E.g. 84 becomes 0.84.
The equivalent fraction is $\frac{84}{100}$. This can be simplified to $\frac{42}{50}$ and $\frac{21}{25}$.

Page 32 — Numbers and Number Lines, Sheet 3

Q1 **–4, –2, 0, 2, 6, 10**

Q2 Left to right:
–1, 3, 11

Q3 a) –3 < 2
b) –1 > –4
c) 0 < 10
d) 0 > –10

Q4 Left to right:
–8, 2, 18
a) **–10 < –5**
b) **0 > –1**

Activity:
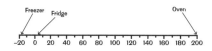

Page 33 — Numbers and Number Lines, Sheet 4

Q1 **5.2, 5.4, 5.6, 6.1, 6.3**

Q2 a) **8.1, 8.7, 9.0**
b) **27.8, 26.6**
c) **–11, –16**
d) **–0.3, –0.8**

Q3 Left to right, above and below line:
–1.6, –0.8, –0.3, 0.6, 1.8

Activity:
For example, a number sequence might be:

-0.8, -0.2, 0.4, 1.0, 1.6
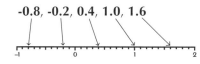

Page 34 — Numbers and Number Lines, Sheet 5

Q1 a) **–1 (kitchen)**
b) **5**

Q2 a) **22 degrees Celsius**
b) **2 degrees Celsius**

Q3 a) **–2 degrees Celsius**
b) Planet Chillon has dropped from 3 degrees to –15, a difference of 18 degrees. Planet Freezon has dropped from –2 degrees to –17, a difference of 15 degrees. **Planet Chillon** has had the greater decrease.

Activity:
Questions similar to those in question 1 should be written, based on child's own castle.

Page 35 — Percentages, Sheet 1

Q1 a) Simon: **35% incorrect**
Helen: **80% correct**
Penny: **50% incorrect**
Tim: **85% correct**
b) 30 ÷ 100 × 50 = **15 words**

Q2 a) **2 squares should be shaded**
b) **You would need to shade 2 more squares to cover 50%.**

Q3 a) **25%**
b) **99%**
c) **56%**
d) **80%**
e) **40%**
f) **42%**

Q4 No. $\frac{1}{4}$ is equivalent to 25% because 1 ÷ 4 × 100 is 25. 19% is less than 25% so $\frac{1}{4}$ is larger than 19%.

Activity:
E.g. a shirt might be 65% polyester and 35% cotton. Make sure the percentages add up to 100%.

Page 36 — Percentages, Sheet 2

Q1 Cat Castle: **29%**
Mousetastic: **28%**
Pet Palace: **76%**
Dave's Dog Shop: **25%**

Q2 a) **1 square should be shaded.**
b) **2 squares should be shaded.**

Q3 20 ÷ 50 × 100 = **40%**

Q4 a) **27%**
b) **90%**
c) **30%**
d) **75%**

ANSWERS

Answers

Activity:
For fractions equivalent to 50%, the bottom number should be twice the top number.

For example, $\frac{1}{2}, \frac{2}{4}, \frac{3}{6}$.

For fractions equivalent to 25%, the bottom number should be four times the top number.

For example, $\frac{1}{4}, \frac{2}{8}, \frac{3}{12}$.

Page 37 — Percentages, Sheet 3

Q1 a) **0.12**
 b) **0.35**
 c) **0.78**
 d) **0.04**

Q2 You should have circled the following fractions:
$\frac{4}{10}, \frac{3}{5}, \frac{2}{3}, \frac{4}{7}, \frac{4}{11}, \frac{2}{8}$.

Q3 a) $250 \div 1000 \times 100 = \textbf{25\%}$
 b) $27 \div 270 \times 100 = \textbf{10\%}$
 c) $11 \div 20 \times 100 = \textbf{55\%}$
 d) $300 \div 500 \times 100 = \textbf{60\%}$

Activity:
Possible answers include; 10p and £1, 1p and 10p, 2p and 20p, 50p and £5.

Page 38 — Proportion and Ratio, Sheet 2

Q1 a) $\frac{1}{3}$ or $\frac{3}{9}$
 b) 15 windows should be shaded.

Q2 a) $56p \times 3 = \textbf{£1.68}$
 b) **Martha will fill about $\frac{1}{4}$ of the bucket with her shells.**

Q3 a) $6 \div 2 = 3$
 $3 \times 3 = \textbf{9 yachts}$
 b) $10 \div 2 = 5$
 $5 \times 3 = \textbf{15 yachts}$

Activity:
E.g. 3 people liked banana milkshake to 2 people who didn't. Using this ratio, in a group of 20, 12 people would like banana milkshake and 8 wouldn't (multiply number of people by 4). Or, in a group of 100, 60 would like banana milkshake and 40 wouldn't (multiply number of people by 20).

Page 39 — Proportion and Ratio, Sheet 3

Q1 a) There should be 6 blue stripes and 9 yellow stripes in the scarf.
 b) 2 in every 5 stripes are coloured **blue**.
 3 in every 5 stripes are coloured yellow.

Q2 a)

Away	Home	Total
3	5	**8**
6	10	**16**
9	15	**24**
12	**20**	**32**
15	**25**	40

 b) **There are 30 away fans.** Using the table to help, double 40 total fans is 80, and double 15 away fans is 30.

Q3 a) $150 \text{ g} \times 2 = \textbf{300 g}$
 b) $600 \text{ ml} \times 2 = \textbf{1200 ml}$

Activity:

Hotdogs	Onions
4	1
8	2
12	3
16	4
20	5

Page 40 — Proportion and Ratio, Sheet 4

Q1 a) $£2.80 \div 7 = \textbf{40p}$
 b) $£120 \div 10 = £12$
 $£12 \times 25 = \textbf{£300}$

Q2 She needs 75 g strawberries because she needs exactly half as much strawberry as orange. 150 g oranges $\div 2 = \textbf{75 g}$

Q3 a) **422**
 b) **446**
 c) **462**

Activity:
Many possible answers. For example, if there are 8 characters and 6 are boys the fraction who are boys would be $\frac{6}{8}$ or $\frac{3}{4}$, and the fraction who are girls would be $\frac{2}{8}$ or $\frac{1}{4}$.

Page 41 — Rounding, Sheet 3

Q1 a) **2000** b) **4000**
 c) **6000** d) **6000**

Q2 a) **5700** b) **2700**
 c) **5800** d) **6800**

Q3 $5327 \rightarrow 5330$
 $5372 \rightarrow 5370$
 $5355 \rightarrow 5360$
 $5318 \rightarrow 5320$

Q4

Height	Nearest 1000 m	Nearest 100 m
8611 m	9000 m	8600 m
8091 m	8000 m	8100 m
1085 m	1000 m	1100 m
4810 m	5000 m	4800 m

150

Answers

Activity:
Any numbers between 2500 and 3499 inclusive will round to 3000 to the nearest 1000.
Any numbers between 2995 and 3004 inclusive will round to 3000 to the nearest 10.

Page 42 — Rounding, Sheet 4

Q1 a) **300**   b) **8500**
   c) **3900**

Q2

Number	to 1 decimal place	to the nearest whole number
14.71	**14.7**	**15**
7.29	**7.3**	**7**
21.98	**22.0**	**22**

Q3

surfboard	to the nearest pound	to the nearest 10p
£23.99	**£24**	**£24.00**
£31.50	**£32**	**£31.50**
£50.25	**£50**	**£50.30**

Activity:
E.g.
Protein: 8.8 g ⇒ **9.0 g**
Carbohydrate: 12.1 g ⇒ **12.0 g**
Fat: 1.2 g ⇒ **1.0 g**
Fibre: 3.8 g ⇒ **4.0 g**

Page 43 — Rounding, Sheet 5

Q1 a) 5.24 → **5.2**
   b) 5.24 → **5**
   c) 7.85 → **7.9**
   d) 7.85 → **8**
   e) 9.53 → **9.5**
   f) 9.53 → **10**

Q2   3.672 → 3.67
     3.267 → 3.27
     3.762 → 3.76
     3.726 → 3.73
     3.276 → 3.28

Q3 a) **£5**
   b) **No. He needs 15p more.**

Activity:
E.g.
Plant pot £3.99 ⇒ £4
Compost £5.25 ⇒ £5
Cactus   £1.95 ⇒ £2
Seeds   £2.19 ⇒ £2
Estimated total = £13
Actual total = £13.38
Difference = 38p

Page 44 — Adding and Subtracting, Sheet 4

Q1 a) **4000**
   b) **2800**
   c) **790**

Q2 a) **£5.50**
   b) **£9.10**
   c) **£1.60**

Q3 a) **330**
   b) **5090**
   c) **930**
   d) **210**

Q4   250 — 170
     640 — 560
     950 — 1030
     1020 — 940

Activity:
Any map can be drawn with roads of different lengths marking different landmarks or buildings.
Route lengths can then be calculated, as shown in the example on the sheet.

Page 45 — Adding and Subtracting, Sheet 5

Q1 a) **3.9**   b) **8.7**
   c) **0.2**   d) **0.7**

Q2 a) **6.4 cm**
   b) **4.2 cm**
   c) **1.7 cm**

Q3   From left to right:
     10.2, 4.6, 6.1, 1.7, 2.2

Q4   **12.7 and 14.3**

Q5   **6.3 and 9.9**

Activity:
E.g.   3 = 0.1 + 2.9
          0.2 + 2.8
          0.3 + 2.7
          0.4 + 2.6 and so on...

Page 46 — Adding and Subtracting, Sheet 6

Q1 a) **6.8**   b) **5.4**
   c) **1.5**   d) **1.9**

Q2 a) **£5.80**
   b) **£3.60**
   c) **£5.10**
   d) **£2.50**

Q3 a) **9.1 cm**
   b) **9.9 cm**
   c) **0.8 cm**

Activity:
Using an A4 sheet:
distance around edge =
29.7 cm + 29.7 + 21.0 cm + 21.0 cm = **101.4 cm**

Page 47 — Adding and Subtracting, Sheet 7

Q1 a) **8.2**   b) **5.7**
   c) **4.3**   d) **0.8**

Q2 a) **2.3 — 6.9**
     3.5 — 5.7
     4.7 — 4.5
     5.9 — 3.3
   b) **2.3 — 11.5**
     3.5 — 12.7
     4.7 — 13.9
     5.9 — 15.1

Q3 a) **4.3** or **four point three**
   b) **9.4** or **nine point four**

Q4   Prawns + cake =
     £4.99 + £4.75 = £9.74
     Spaghetti + sandwich =
     £6.99 + £3.50 = £10.49
     £9.74 is closer to £10 than £10.49, so **prawns and cake** is the answer.

Activity:
E.g. £7.99 + £8.99 + £10.49 =
     £27.47

Answers

Page 48 — Checking Calculations, Sheet 4

Q1 **5, 10, 10, 5**

Q2 Paul: **£5.94**
Amy: **£13.88**

Q3 a) **200 ÷ 50 = 4**
Jim's statement seems about right.
b) **52 × 4 = 208**
Jim is wrong. There aren't enough seats.

Activity:
E.g. £1.39 ⇒ £1
£2.99 ⇒ £3
£0.95 ⇒ £1
£4.29 ⇒ £4
Total: £9.62   Estimate: £9

Page 49 — Checking Calculations, Sheet 5

Q1 For a) and b) two of any of the following answers:
14 + 13 = 27
27 − 14 = 13
27 − 13 = 14

Q2 a) **2**
b) **9**
c) **42**
d) **15**

Q3 **583 − 318**

Q4 a) **8 × 4 = 32**
b) **32 = 4 × 8**
c) **32 ÷ 8 = 4**

Q5 **1700 − 900 = 800**

Activity:
For example, the distances might be:
15.7 miles, 6.3 miles, 10.2 miles, 0.6 miles and 2.9 miles.
An estimated total might be:
36 miles

Page 50 — Checking Calculations, Sheet 6

Q1 Rounded figures and estimated answer:
350 ÷ 10 = 35
Inverse calculation to check Tom's answer:
44 × 8 = 352
or **8 × 44 = 352**

Q2 a)

Day of week	Number of dinners	Rounded to the nearest 10
Monday	367	370
Tuesday	219	220
Wednesday	402	400
Thursday	384	380
Friday	421	420

b) 370 + 220 = **590**
c) 367 + 219 = **586**
d) Either of the following:
586 − 219 = 367
586 − 367 = 219

Activity:
For example, the number of windows and chairs might be:
9 and 23.
The total would be:
32
Calculations to check this might be:
23 + 9 = 32
32 − 9 = 23
32 − 23 = 9

Page 51 — Checking Calculations, Sheet 7

Q1 a) **231 + 725 = 956** or
725 + 231 = 956
Missing number is **956**
b) **974 − 256 = 718**
Missing number is **718**
c) **67 + 15 = 82** or
15 + 67 = 82
Missing number is **82**
d) **436 − 191 = 245**
Missing number is **245**

Q2 a) **800 ÷ 40 = 20**
b) **Less than 20, because 798 is a smaller number than 800, being divided by 41 which is a bigger number than 40.**
c) **45 × 30 = 1350**

Q3 **Yes. Because two odd numbers added together should make an even number.**

Activity:
For example, a list of numbers divisible by 2 might be:
1482, 36, 984, 7892, 88
A pattern would be that all numbers that are divisible by 2 are even — or the last digit is always divisible by two.

Page 52 — Checking Calculations, Sheet 8

Q1 a) **37 − 14 = £23**
b) Any one of the following:
36.60 − 22.80 = 13.80
13.80 + 22.80 = 36.60
22.80 + 13.80 = 36.60
c) Using rounding they would cost:
20 × 1.10 = **£22.00**
She could afford them.
d) Using the exact figures they would cost:
21 × 1.11 = **£23.31**
She can't afford them.

Q2 a) The last digit is 8 — which is even. Numbers divisible by 2 have an even last digit.
b) **The sum of the digits is 11 — which isn't divisible by 9. Numbers divisible by 9 have a sum of digits divisible by 9.**
c) **The last two digits are 40 — which is divisible by 4. The last two digits of multiples of 4 are divisible by 4.**
d) **The last digit is 5. The last digit of multiples of 5 is 5 or 0.**

Activity:
For example, the time spent asleep in one night might be 513 minutes. This could be rounded to 510 minutes.
Number of minutes slept in a week might be:
510 × 7 = 3570 or 500 × 7 = 3500
Number of minutes slept in a year might be:
3570 × 52 = 185640 or
3500 × 50 = 175000

152

Answers

Page 53 — Doubling and Halving, Sheet 3

Q1 a) **52**
b) **220**
c) **31**
d) **180**

Q2 a) Either:
190 + 190 = 380p or
190 × 2 = 380p
b) Either:
150 + 150 = 300p or
150 × 2 = 300p
c) **18 ÷ 2 = 9p**
9 × 10 = 90p
d) **26 ÷ 2 = 13p**
13 × 10 = 130p

Q3 a) 240 + 240 = **480** or
240 × 2 = **480**
b) 240 ÷ 2 = **120**

Activity:
For example, there might be 554
students in a school.
Doubling that would make **1108**.
Halving it would make **277**.

Page 54 — Doubling and Halving, Sheet 4

Q1 a) **7.6**
b) **7.2**
c) **8.4**
d) **8.2**
e) **0.6**
f) **7.8**

Q2 a) **37**
b) **3.7**

Q3 a) **48**
b) **4.8**

Q4 a) **3.4**
b) **4.1**
c) **0.1**
d) **7.2**

Q5 a) **7.6**
b) **9.6**
c) **19.4**
d) **1.0**

Activity:
For example, the spare change
might come to:
£13.72
Double this would be:
£27.44
Half of this would be:
£6.86

Page 55 — Doubling and Halving, Sheet 5

Q1 a) **4.2, 8.4, 16.8, 33.6**
b) **44.4, 22.2, 11.1, 5.55**

Q2 a) Either:
4.2 + 4.2 = 8.4 cm or
4.2 × 2 = 8.4 cm
b) **6.7 ÷ 2 = 3.35 cm**

Q3 a) 92.4 + **92.4 = 184.8 cm**
b) 92.4 ÷ **2 = 46.2 cm**

Activity:
For example, the pencil case might
be:
32.6 cm
Double this would be **65.2 cm**
Half of this would be **16.3 cm**

Page 56 — Doubling and Halving, Sheet 6

Q1 a) **1.5**
b) **0.47**
c) **12.8**
d) **1.9**

Q2 **10.0 – 6.2 = 3.8**

Q3 a) Either:
18.5 + 18.5 = **£37.00** or
18.5 × 2 = **£37.00**
Yes he does have enough.
b) He'll need:
42 ÷ 2 = £21
So he'll need to save:
21 – 18.50 = **£2.50**

Q4 **double 2.1 = half of 8.4**
6.6 ÷ 2 = 5.5 – 2.2
3.2 + 4.4 = 2 × 3.8

Activity:
For example, it might be:
41.7 cm
A calculation to double this would
be either:
41.7 + 41.7 = 83.4 or
41.7 × 2 = 83.4 cm
A calculation to halve this would
be:
41.7 ÷ 2 = 20.85 cm

Page 57 — Factors and Multiples, Sheet 1

Q1 **1, 2, 3, 4, 6, 8** and **12**

Q2 b) **3 × 4** = 12
c) **6 × 2** = 12
(the order doesn't matter)

Q3 a) The factors of 15 are **1**, **3**, **5**
and **15**
b) The factors of 36 are **1, 2,
3, 4, 6, 9, 12, 18,** and **36**

Q4 **12, 24** and **36**

Activity:
83: This can be worked out by
realising that the common multiples
of 3 and 4 are all in the 12 times
table, and that there are 83 12s in
1000.
This can be done by chunking into
120 = 10, 240 = 20, 360 = 30 etc.

Page 58 — Factors and Multiples, Sheet 2

Q1 a) **1 × 24** = 24, **12 × 2** = 24, **6
× 4** = 24 and **3 × 8** = 24
b) **1 × 38** = 38 and
19 × 2 = 38
c) **1 × 17** = 17

Q2 **15, 30, 45** and **60**

Q3 a) **1, 2, 4, 8, 16** and **32**
b) **1, 2, 3, 4, 6, 8, 9, 12, 18, 24,
36** and **72**
c) **1, 2, 3, 4, 6, 8, 12, 16, 24,
32, 48** and **96**

Q4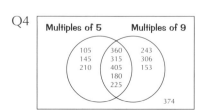

ANSWERS

Answers

Activity:
Any multiple of 42p, e.g. 84p,
£1.26, £42

Page 59 — Factors and Multiples, Sheet 3

Q1 **13, 19, 31, 53, 79** and **83**

Q2 a) 42 = **1 × 42** OR **2 × 21** OR
3 × 14 OR **6 × 7**.
42 is **not prime**.
b) 23 = **1 × 23**.
23 is **prime**.
c) 17 = **1 × 17**.
17 is **prime**.
d) 29 = **1 × 29**.
29 is **prime**.

Q3 a) 77 = **11 × 7**
b) 12 = **2 × 2 × 3**
c) 18 = **2 × 3 × 3**

Q4
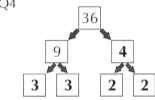

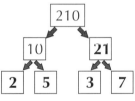

(or **5 × 2** and **7 × 3**)

Activity:
Using the three largest prime
numbers: **97 x 89 x 83 = 716539**

Page 60 — Multiplication and Division, Sheet 7

Q1 a) **7**
b) **54**
c) **8**
d) **9**
e) **8**
f) **8**

Q2 a) 21 − 1 = 20
20 ÷ 5 = **4**
b) 4 × 6 = 24
24 + 3 = **27**
c) 6 × 6 = 36
36 ÷ 4 = **9**

Q3 a) **24**
b) **2**

Activity:
1, 2, 3, 5, 7, 11, 13, 17, 19

Page 61 — Multiplication and Division, Sheet 8

Q1 a) 24 ÷ 6 = **4**
4 × 6 = 24
b) 63 ÷ 7 = **9**
9 × 7 = 63
c) 32 ÷ 8 = **4**
4 × 8 = 32 or 8 × **4** = 32

Q2 a) **80**
b) **800**
c) **180**
d) **1800**

Q3 a) **30**
b) **70**
c) **5**
d) **4**

Q4 Multiples of 20 = **60, 120,
160, 200, 240**
Multiples of 30 = **60, 120,
150, 240**
Multiples of 40 = **120, 160,
200, 240**
Multiples of 50 = **150, 200**

Activity:
E.g. 6 × 6 = 36, 5 × 7 = 35,
70 ÷ 2 = 35, 96 ÷ 3 = 32.

Page 62 — Multiplication and Division, Sheet 9

Q1

	÷2	÷3	÷4	÷5	÷6	÷7	÷8	÷9	÷10
24	12	8	6	X	4	X	3	X	X
36	18	12	9	X	6	X	X	4	X
35	X	X	X	7	X	5	X	X	X
48	24	16	12	X	8	X	6	X	X
56	28	X	14	X	X	8	7	X	X

Q2 a) **18**
b) **28**
c) **40**
d) **54**
e) **56**
f) **48**

Q3 a) **180**
b) **280**
c) **400**
d) **5400**
e) **5600**
f) **4800**

Activity:
E.g. David Ryan has 5 letters in his
first name and 4 letters in his second
name, so his lucky number is 2:
5 × 4 = 20, 2 + 0 = 2.

Page 63 — Multiplication and Division, Sheet 10

Q1 a) **3**
b) **5.6**
c) **2.5**
d) **2.8**
e) **2.8**
f) **2.4**

Q2 a) **0.6**
b) **0.6**
c) **0.7**
d) **0.7**
e) **0.6**
f) **0.7**

Q3 a) From top to bottom:
2, 3, 4
b) From top to bottom:
0.9, 0.2, 0.5

Q4 a) £4.20 ÷ 7 = **£0.60**
b) £0.90 × 9 = **£8.10**

Activity:
E.g. £4.20 can be shared equally
between groups of 1, 2, 3, 4, 5, 6, 7,
10, 12, 14, 15 and 20 people.

Page 64 — Calculators, Sheet 2

Q1 a) **46,292**
b) **143**
c) **25,346**
d) **920**
e) **697**
f) **−4145**

Q2 £14 ÷ 5 = **£2.80**

Answers

Q3 a) **£1.22**
b) **£1.22**
c) **79p**
d) **£84.08**
e) **£1.99**
f) **£157.20**

Q4 a) **−142**
b) **−9**
c) **79**
d) **15**

Q5 £10.92 ÷ 13 = 84
84 ÷ 7 = **12 weeks**

Activity:
Many possible answers depending on your chosen adverts.

Page 65 — Calculators, Sheet 3

Q1 a) **1.69**
b) **31.25**
c) **6.25**
d) **5.45**

Q2 a) **68**
b) **204**
c) **79**
d) **237**
e) **22**
f) **110**
g) **21**
h) **147**

Q3 a) **9 metres and 90 cm (or 990 cm)**
b) **10 cm**

Q4 a) **187.2 cm or 1.872 m**
b) **1.3 m**
c) **11.722 km**
d) **28.61 m**
e) **10.868 m**
f) **1.212 m or 121.2 cm**

Activity:
Many possible answers depending on the length of your stride. For example if your stride is 60 cm, you would walk 1.2 km in 2000 steps and 1.8 km in 3000 steps.

Page 66 — Calculators, Sheet 4

Q1 a) **3.675 kg**
b) **2 kg or 2000 g**
c) **400 g or 0.4 kg**
d) **2.03 kg**
e) **500 g or 0.5 kg**

Q2 a) **0.25**
b) **39**
c) **1030**
d) **927**

Q3
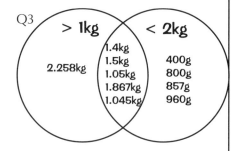

Q4 500 ÷ 7 = 71.429
71.429 × 30 = **2.143 kg**

Activity:
Many possible answers depending on your arm span. For example, if your arm span is 1.5 m, you divide 168 m by 1.5 m, giving an answer of 112 arm spans.

Page 67 — Calculators, Sheet 5

Q1 a) **43.75**
b) **13.92**
c) **33.8541**

Q2 27 × 6p = £1.62
£2 − £1.62 = **38p**

Q3
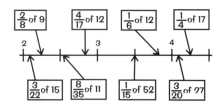

Q4 156 ÷ 12 = 13
13 × 16 = **208 girls**

Activity:
Many possible answers.
For example, 01234 432323:
0 + 1 + 2 + 3 + 4
+ 4 + 3 + 2 + 3 + 2 + 3 = 27
Average is 27 ÷ 11 = 2.45

Page 68 — Calculators, Sheet 6

Q1 a) £1.32 × 2.7 = **£3.56**
b) 43.2 ÷ 1.8 = **24**

Q2 £3.57 × 13 = £46.41
£50 − £46.41 = **£3.59**

Q3 a) **16**
b) **32**
c) **4**
d) **−197**
e) **−278**

Q4 **32,910**

Activity:
2 × (3 + 6) = 18 and (2 × 3) + 6 = 12. If you take out the brackets, the calculator gives an answer of 12 because it works out the multiplication and then the addition, using the BODMAS rule.

Page 69 — Mental Maths, Sheet 4

Q1 a) **12**
b) **64**
c) **28**
d) **35**
e) **12**
f) **39**

Q2 **41 and 29, 25 and 37**

Q3 a) 19 + 35 =
20 + 35 − 1 = **54**
b) 31 + 17 =
30 + 17 + 1 = **48**
c) 78 + 20 =
80 + 20 − 2 = **98**

Q4 a) **7p**
b) **57**

Answers

Activity:
E.g. some of the phone numbers might be:

555 729
555 646
555 984
555 812

Adding the last two digits the closest to 100 they could get without going over would be:
84 + 12 = **96**

Page 70 — Mental Maths, Sheet 5

Q1 b) 20 × 3 = **60**
(double 10 × 3)
c) 50 × 5 = **250**
(5 × 5 × 10)

Q2 a) 5030 − 2997 =
5030 − 3000 + 3 =
2033
b) 2003 − 900 =
2000 − 900 + 3 =
1103

Q3 a) 15 × 5 = **75p**
b) 68 ÷ 4 = **17p**
c) 24 × 4 = **96p**

Q4 a) 11 × 25 =
10 × 25 + 25 =
275
b) 2834 + 2999 =
2834 + 3000 − 1 =
5833
c) 14 × 4 =
10 × 4 + 4 × 4 =
56
(A different method can be used as long as they arrive at the same answer.)

Activity:
53, 54, 55

Page 71 — Mental Maths, Sheet 6

Q1 a) 3 × 7 = **21**
b) 30 × 7 = **210**
c) 0.3 × 7 = **2.1**
d) 2 × 8 = **16**
e) 20 × 8 = **160**
f) 0.2 × 8 = **1.6**
g) 6 × 7 = **42**
h) 60 × 7 = **420**
i) 0.6 × 7 = **4.2**

Q2   5.00 − 2.60 = 2.40
2.40 ÷ 2 = **£1.20**

Q3 Circle **0.01** and **9.99**

Q4 a) 36 ÷ 4 = 9, so
3.6 ÷ 4 = **0.9 m**
b) 36 ÷ 6 = 6, so
3.6 ÷ 6 = **0.6 m**
c) 3.6 − 1.1 − 1.1 = **1.4 m**

Q5   60 × 6 = 360, and
7 × 6 = 42, so
67 × 6 = 402, so
6.7 × 6 = **40.2**

Activity:
To get exactly 517 you could do 250 × 2 = 500
4 × 5 = 20
20 − 3 = 17
500 + 17 = 517
or, 250 × 2 = 500
3 × 4 = 12
12 + 5 = 17
500 + 17 = 517

Page 72 — Multiply by 10, 100 and 1000, Sheet 3

Q1   **84**

Q2 a) **100**
b) **1570**
c) **23**
d) **100**

Q3 a) **4500**
b) **562**
c) **270**
d) **86**

Q4   680 ÷ 10 = **68**

Activity:
Examples for 6 × 7 = 42:
6 × 70 = 420,
6 × 700 = 4200,
600 × 7 = 4200,
60 × 70 = 4200.
Examples for 3 × 8 = 24:
30 × 8 = 240
3 × 80 = 240
3 × 800 = 2400
300 × 8 = 2400
30 × 80 = 2400.

Page 73 — Multiply by 10, 100 and 1000, Sheet 4

Q1 a) **10**
b) **10**
c) **100**

Q2 a) **250**
b) **1000**
c) **4.2**
d) **564**
e) **7360**
f) **10**
g) **16**

Q3   2.5 cm × 100 = **250 cm** or **2.5 m**

Q4   61 × 10 = 610
610 × 100 = **61 000**

Activity:
For example, one cake needs 200 g butter, 150 g sugar and 100 g flour. 100 cakes would need 20 000 g or 20 kg butter, 15 000 g or 15 kg sugar and 10 000 g or 10 kg flour. To make a tenth of one cake, you would need 20 g butter, 15 g sugar and 10 g flour.

Page 74 — Multiply by 10, 100 and 1000, Sheet 5

Q1 a) **100**
b) **10**
c) **1000**

Q2 a) **7500**
b) **100**
c) **21**
d) **0.82**

Answers

Q3 **46**

Q4 a) 73 kg = 73 000 g
   73 000 g ÷ 100 = **730 g** or
   0.73 kg
   b) 10 chickens eat:
   730 g × 10 = 7300 g
   7300 g = 7.3 kg
   100 chickens eat:
   7.3 kg × 10 = 73 kg
   110 chickens eat:
   73 kg + 7.3 kg = **80.3 kg**

Activity:
For example, if you choose 45:
45 × 10 = 450.
45 ÷ 10 = 4.5
450 + 4.5 = 454.5.
The second number replaces the 0 in the first answer so that the digits of the original number are repeated.

Page 75 — Using Fractions, Sheet 4

Q1 There are 30 ÷ 5 = **6 boys**.
   So number of girls is
   6 × 4 = **24 girls**.
   (or 30 − 6 = 24)

Q2 a) 24 g ÷ 8 = 3 g
   3 g × 3 = **9 g**
   b) 21 cm ÷ 7 = 3 cm
   3 cm × 2 = **6 cm**

Q3 Joanne: 32 ÷ 8 = 4
   4 × 5 = **20 points**
   Lee: 32 ÷ 8 = **4 points**.

Q4 Sweets: 50p ÷ 10 = **5p**
   Pencil: 50p ÷ 5 = **10p**
   Stickers: 50p ÷ 10 = 5p
      5p × 3 = **15p**
   Comic: 50p ÷ 5 = 10p
      10p × 2 = **20p**

Activity:
Many possible answers. Make sure that the fraction sentences are sensible.

Page 76 — Using Fractions, Sheet 5

Q1 b) 120 ÷ 3 = 40
      40 × 2 = **80**.
   c) 120 ÷ 10 = 12
      12 × 7 = **84**.

Q2 Using the hint,
   5% is half of 10%.

   10% of 60 = 60 ÷ 10 = 6
   6 ÷ 2 = **3**
   (the answer should be written in the triangle).

   10% of 140 = 140 ÷ 10 = 14
   14 ÷ 2 = **7**
   (the answer should be written in the oval).

   10% of 120 = 120 ÷ 10 = 12
   12 ÷ 2 = **6**
   (the answer should be written in the star).

Q3 First row:
   20 m ÷ 5 = 4 m
   4 m × 3 = **12 m**
   40 kg ÷ 5 = 8 kg
   8 kg × 3 = **24 kg**
   80 mins ÷ 5 = 16 mins
   16 m × 3 = **48 mins**

   Second row:
   25% is the same as $\frac{1}{4}$.
   40 kg ÷ 4 = **10 kg**
   80 mins ÷ 4 = **20 mins**
   £1.20 = 120p.
   120p ÷ 4 = **30p**

Activity:
One fifth of 35 = **7**
One fifth of 100 = **20**
One fifth of 75 = **15**
One fifth of 150 = **30**
One fifth of 60 = **12**

Any number in the **5 times table** that is **smaller than 75** will give whole number answers less than 15. Not including the numbers given above, these are:
5, 10, 15, 20, 25, 30, 40, 45, 50, 55, 65 and **70**.
Choose any three of these numbers.

Page 77 — Using Fractions, Sheet 6

Q1 a) 12 ÷ 3 = $\frac{1}{3}$ of 12

   b) 18 × $\frac{1}{6}$ = 18 ÷ 6

Q2 There are 4 people sharing the pizzas. They will each get 5 ÷ 4 = $1\frac{1}{4}$ pizzas.

Q3 39 ÷ 4 = $9\frac{3}{4}$ = **9.75**

   58 ÷ 5 = $11\frac{3}{5}$ = **11.6**

   63 ÷ 10 = $6\frac{3}{10}$ = **6.3**

   In the last column, $3\frac{1}{4}$ has a 4 in the denominator of the fraction. This means it has been divided by 4.

   $3\frac{1}{4}$ × 4 = 13.

   So $3\frac{1}{4}$ = **13 : 4 = 3.25**

Q4 The correct answers are:
   $\frac{7}{8}$ of 64 = 56

   90% of 60 = 54

   $\frac{5}{11}$ of 121 = 55

Q5 a) 55% of 120 m
      = 120 m ÷ 100 × 55
      = **66 m**
   b) 70% of 230 g
      = 230 g ÷ 100 × 70
      = **161 g**

Activity:
Many possible answers.
To find 15% of a number, use:
Number ÷ 100 × 15
To find 35% of a number, use:
Number ÷ 100 × 35
To find 65% of a number, use:
Number ÷ 100 × 65
Write the answers as decimals.

To find $\frac{4}{5}$ of a number, use:
Number ÷ 5 × 4

To find $\frac{3}{8}$ of a number, use:
Number ÷ 8 × 3

To find $\frac{7}{10}$ of a number, use:
Number ÷ 10 × 7
Write your answers as fractions.

Answers

Page 78 — Written Adding and Subtracting, Sheet 3

Q1 a) **675**   b) **839**   c) **591**

Q2   845 − 386 = **459**

Q3   £2.25 + £0.12 + £1.95
     = **£4.32**

Q4 a) 2**46** + 1**54** = 400
   b) **9**42 − 237 = 705
   c) **134** + 39**4** = 528
   d) **787** − 1**26** = 661

Activity:
Largest difference
   = 634 − 342 = **292**
Smallest total = 342 + 478 = **820**

Page 79 — Written Adding and Subtracting, Sheet 4

Q1 a) **394**   b) **4.19**   c) 372
   d) **143.9**

Q2 a)   1.07   b)   27.8
       + 2.85   − 2.5
       ——————   ——————
        3.92   25.3

   c)   83.6
       + 2.19
       ——————
        85.79

Q3   £27.16 + £27.16 = **£54.32**

Q4   84 + 198 = 282
     300 − 282 = **18 nails**

Activity:
E.g. **20** + **90** = 110
     60 + 80 = 140
     50 + 50 = 100

Page 80 — Written Adding and Subtracting, Sheet 5

Q1 a)

```
        [ 33 ]
     [ 16 ][ 17 ]
   [ 6 ][ 10 ][ 7 ]
```

   b)

```
        [ 220 ]
     [ 145 ][ 75 ]
   [ 85 ][ 60 ][ 15 ]
```

c)

```
        [ 11.1 ]
     [ 4.8 ][ 6.3 ]
   [ 1.2 ][ 3.6 ][ 2.7 ]
```

d)

```
        [ 85 ]
     [ 41 ][ 44 ]
   [ 15 ][ 26 ][ 18 ]
```

Q2   28.31 − 15.06 = **13.25**

Q3 a)   37   b)   105
          425   20
        + 505   + 235
        ——————   ——————
          967   360

   c)   789
         52
       + 17
       ——————
        858

Q4   172 − 96 = 76
     76 − 25 = **51**

Activity:
E.g. **100** + **35** + **15** = 150
     96 + **28** + **26** = 150

Page 81 — Written Adding and Subtracting, Sheet 6

Q1 a) **636**   b) **13.29**   c) **1232**
   d) **90.97**

Q2   162.8 + 25.7 + 309.4
     = **497.9**

Q3 a)

25	30	**11**	(66)
50	**15**	26	(91)
16	42	35	(93)
(91)	(87)	(72)	

   b)

45	11	26	(**82**)
17	58	**33**	(108)
61	**23**	75	(159)
(123)	(92)	(134)	

Q4   58 + 93 + 14 = 165
     437 − 165 = **272 pages**

Activity:
E.g. the books might have **293**, **385** and **417** pages.
The total number of pages would be:
293 + 385 + 417 = 1095

Page 82 — Written Multiplying and Dividing, Sheet 4

Q1 a) 80 + 24 = **104**
   b) 70 × 5 = **350**
      4 × 5 = **20**
      350 + 20 = **370**
   c) **50 × 3 = 150**
      7 × 3 = 21
      150 + 21 = **171**

Q2 a) 79 ÷ 5
      = 50 ÷ 5 + **29 ÷ 5**
      = 10 + 5 r4 = **15 r 4**
   b) 81 ÷ 6
      = **60 ÷ 6 + 21 ÷ 6**
      = **10 + 3 r3 = 13 r3**
      (Any sensible, correct partitioning is acceptable, e.g. 72 ÷ 6 + 9 ÷ 6.)

Q3 a) 96 = 60 + 36
      60 ÷ 6 = 10
      36 ÷ 6 = 6
      10 + 6 = **16p**
   b) 25 = 20 + 5
      20 × 9 = 180
      5 × 9 = 45
      180 + 45 = **225 m**

Activity:
Possible question where answer is rounded down to 9:
"How many 8p sweets can you buy with 74p?"
Possible question where answer is rounded up to 10:
"A box can store 8 hats. How many boxes are needed for 74 hats?"

158

Answers

Page 83 — Written Multiplying and Dividing, Sheet 5

Q1 a) $300 \times 8 = \textbf{2400}$
$40 \times 8 = \textbf{320}$
$5 \times 8 = \textbf{40}$
$2400 + 320 + 40 = \textbf{2760}$

b) $10 \times 26 = \textbf{260}$
$4 \times 20 = \textbf{80}$
$4 \times 6 = \textbf{24}$
$260 + 80 + 24 = \textbf{364}$

c) E.g. calculate 53×9, then divide the answer by 10.
$50 \times 9 = 450$, and $3 \times 9 = 27$
$450 + 27 = 477$
So $5.3 \times 9 = 477 \div 10 = \textbf{47.7}$

Q2 a) $8)\overline{928}$
$-\underline{800}$ (100×8)
128
$-\underline{80}$ (10×8)
48
$-\underline{48}$ (6×8)
0 $\overline{100 + 10 + 6 = 116}$

116 complete boxes

b) $4)\overline{766}$
$-\underline{400}$ (100×4)
366
$-\underline{360}$ (90×4)
6
$-\underline{4}$ (1×4)
2 $\overline{100 + 90 + 1 = 191}$

They get £**191** each.
There is £**2** left over.

Activity:
Many possible answers, including
$5.4 \times 6 = 32.4$, $5.6 \times 4 = 22.4$,
$6.4 \times 5 = 32$.

Page 84 — Written Multiplying and Dividing, Sheet 6

Q1 a) $700 \times 9 = \textbf{6300}$
$20 \times 9 = \textbf{180}$
$4 \times 9 = \textbf{36}$
$6300 + 180 + 36 = \textbf{6516}$

b) $53 \times 10 = \textbf{530}$
$50 \times 7 = \textbf{350}$
$3 \times 7 = \textbf{21}$
$530 + 350 + 21 = \textbf{901}$

c) E.g. calculate 368×9, then divide the answer by 10.
$300 \times 9 = 2700$
$60 \times 9 = 540$
$8 \times 9 = 72$
$2700 + 540 + 72 = 3312$
$3312 \div 10 = \textbf{331.2}$

Q2 b) $6)\overline{337}$
$-\underline{300}$ (50×6)
37
$-\underline{36}$ (6×6)
1
$50 + 6\ r1 = 56$ **r1** $\rightarrow$ **O**

c) $4)\overline{928}$
$-\underline{800}$ (200×4)
128
$-\underline{120}$ (30×4)
8
$-\underline{8}$ (2×4)
0
$200 + 30 + 2\ r0 = 232$ **r0** $\rightarrow$ **S**

d) $8)\overline{829}$
$-\underline{800}$ (100×8)
29
$-\underline{24}$ (3×8)
5
$100 + 3\ r5 = 103$ **r5** $\rightarrow$ **T**

Word = **POST**

Activity:
Many possible answers. For example, the oldest person might be 68 and the child might be 9.
$60 \times 9 = 540$
$8 \times 9 = 72$
$540 + 72 = 612$
There might be 4 people in the family.
$4)\overline{6^21\ ^12}$ → 153

Page 85 — Written Multiplying and Dividing, Sheet 7

Q1 a) E.g. calculate $99 \div 3$, then divide the answer by 10.
$99 \div 3 = 33$
So $9.9 \div 3 = \textbf{3.3}$

b) $5)\overline{2^23^37^25}$ → 475

c) E.g. calculate $148 \div 4$, then divide the answer by 10.
$4)\overline{1^14^28}$ → 37
So $14.8 \div 4 = \textbf{3.7}$

Q2 $6 \times 3.99 = 23.94$
$4 \times 1.50 = 6$
$23.94 + 6 = \textbf{£29.94}$

Q3 a) E.g. calculate $1032 \div 6$, then divide the answer by 10.
$6)\overline{1^10^43^12}$ → 172
My number was **17.2**.

b) E.g. calculate $48 \div 3$, then divide the answer by 10.
$3)\overline{4^18}$ → 16
Each person is **1.6 m** tall.

Activity:
Many possible answers. For example, if you are 148 cm tall and your little finger measures 4 cm, you would work out 148 cm ÷ 4 cm:
$4)\overline{1^14^28}$ → 37 Answer = 37

Page 86 — 2D Shapes, Sheet 3

Q1 There are:
4 rectangles
12 triangles
3 pentagons
3 circles

Q2 a) Square — **4 equal sides, 4 right angles.**

b) Equilateral triangle — **3 equal sides, no right angles.**

c) Regular pentagon — **5 equal sides, no right angles.**

Q3 Many possible answers. For example:

An isosceles triangle (2 equal sides)

ANSWERS

Answers

A pentagon

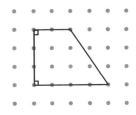

A 4 sided shape with only two right angles

Activity:
Many possible answers.
For example:

Page 87 — 2D Shapes, Sheet 4

Q1 a)

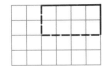

b)

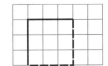

c) Many possible answers.
For example:

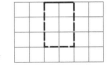

Q2 a) **Regular pentagon.**

b) **Kite or parallelogram**

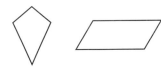

c) **Octagon**

Q3 a) **Equilateral triangle**
b) **Right angled triangle**
c) **Isosceles triangle**
d) **Scalene triangle**

Activity:
Many possible answers. Make sure your triangles are labelled correctly. Use the descriptions on the worksheet to check.

Page 88 — 2D Shapes, Sheet 5

Q1 Shape A — **Perpendicular**
Shape B — **Neither**
Shape C — **Parallel**
Shape D — **Perpendicular**
Shape E — **Parallel**
Shape F — **Parallel**

Q2 a) **Square, rectangle, parallelogram or diamond.**

b) **Trapezium**

c) **Right angled triangle**

d) **Regular hexagon**

Activity:
Many possible answers. The meanings of parallel and perpendicular are given at the top of the worksheet.

Page 89 — 3D Shapes, Sheet 3

Q1 a) **Square-based pyramid**
b) **Cylinder**
c) **Triangular prism**

Q2 The picture should be coloured like this:

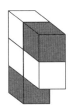

Q3 **Net a)** and **net b)** should be circled.

Activity
To make your own cube, you could use net b) from Q3 and put on tabs like this:

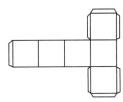

Each side of the cube should measure 5 cm.

Page 90 — 3D Shapes, Sheet 4

Q1 Diagrams **a)** and **d)** are nets of cuboids. They should be circled.

Answers

Q2 a) **Triangle-based pyramid**
Net:

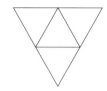

b) **Triangular prism**
Net:

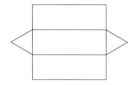

Q3   Faces: **8**
Edges: **12**
Vertices: **6**

Activity:
There are many possible ways to make a net for this triangular prism. For example:

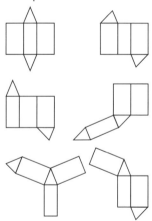

Page 91 — 3D Shapes, Sheet 5

Q1 a) The shaded faces of the cube are **perpendicular** to each other.

b) The shaded faces of the cylinder are **parallel** to each other.

c) The highlighted edges of the hexagonal prism are **parallel** to each other.

Q2 a) There are **2** edges parallel to the shaded edge.

b) There are **4** faces perpendicular to the shaded face.

c) There are **4** edges parallel to the shaded edge.

Q3   Sam's shape is a **cuboid** or a **cube**.
Ayesha's shape is a **pentagonal prism**.

Activity:
Many possible answers.   Make sure that parallel and perpendicular faces and edges are correctly coloured.

Page 92 — Angles, Sheet 3

Q1 a) **370°**

b) **360°**

c) **325°**

a) and **c)** are wrong.
The angles don't add up to 360°

Q2 a)

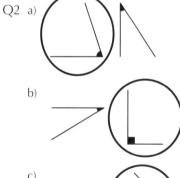

b)

c)

Q3   **B A D C E**

Q4

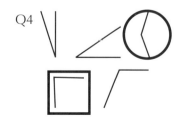

Activity:
Many possible answers.
For example:

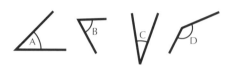

Smallest to largest: **C A B D**

Page 93 — Angles, Sheet 4

Q1 a) 55° (Accept **50°** or **60°**)

b) 88° (Accept **90°**)

c) 123°
(Accept **110°**, **120°** or **130°**)

Q2 (Accept answers 2° either way:)

a) **52°** and **90°**

b) **130°** and **35°**

c) **112°** and **168°**

Q3

Activity:
For example:
a) I drew this for 90°:

with a protractor it measures 92°, so I was 2° out.

Page 94 — Angles, Sheet 5

Q1 a) x = **70°**

b) x = **82°**

c) x = **47°**

Q2 a) **D**

b) **B**

Q3

Answers

Activity:
Many possible answers.
For example:

I measured angle *a* as 56°,
and angle *b* as 46°.
I calculated angle *c* as
180 − 56 − 46 = **78°**
I measured the angle at 79° so I was
very close.

Page 95 — Calculating Angles, Sheet 1

Q1   180° − 30° = **150°**

Q2 a) a = 180° − 135° = **45°**
    b) b = 180° − 60° = **120°**

Q3   180° − (90° + 35°) = **55°**

Q4 a) c = 180° − (40° + 40°)
        = **100°**
    b) d = 180° − (50° + 40°
        + 20°) = **70°**

Activity:
The corners will fit exactly along the
line with any triangle. The angles in
a triangle add up to 180°.

Page 96 — Calculating Angles, Sheet 2

Q1 a) a = **33°** (allow 32° − 34°)
    b) b = **99°** (allow 98° − 100°)
    c) c = **48°** (allow 47° − 49°)
        The angles add up to 180°.

Q2   d = 180° ÷ 6 = **30°**

Q3   If e is 2 × f, then f must be
        60° (180° ÷ 3)
        So e = 2 × 60° = **120°**

Activity:
The cake can be divided into any
number of pieces that is a factor of
180.
The factors of 180 are: 2, 3, 4, 5, 6,
9, 10, 12, 15, 18, 20, 30, 36, 45,
60, 90. Though in practice, slices of
less than 15° would be very tricky to
cut.

Page 97 — Calculating Angles, Sheet 3

Q1 a) a = 180° − (90° + 40°)
        = **50°**
    b) b = 180° − (50° + 30°)
        = **100°**
    c) c = 180° − (80° + 70°)
        = **30°**

Q2 a) 180° − 10° = 170°
        d = 170° ÷ 2 = **85°**
    b) e = **45°**
        f = 180° − (45° + 45°) = **90°**

Q3 a) 360° − (80° + 70° + 140°)
        = **70°**
    b) 360° − (60° + 50° + 110°
        + 30°) = **110°**

Q4   360° ÷ 5 = **72°**

Activity:
The angle between the hands at
5 o'clock is 150°.

Page 98 — Coordinates, Sheet 3

Q1   **south-west**

Q2 a), b), c)

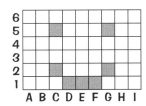

Q3 a) **north-west**
    b) **north-east**
    c) Go **4** squares in a **south-west**
        direction.

Activity:
e.g. the map could be based on a
holiday.

Page 99 — Coordinates, Sheet 4

Q1 a) **(2,5)**
    b) **(7,4)**
    c) **(10,5)**
    d) **(5,1)**

Q2 a)

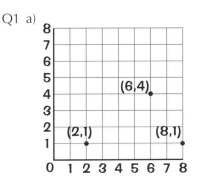

    b) **rectangle**

Q3   right-angled triangle

Activity:
E.g. (2,1), (3,7) and (5,4) are the
vertices of a scalene triangle.
(2,2), (6,2) and (4,7) are the vertices
of an isosceles triangle.

Page 100 — Coordinates, Sheet 5

Q1 a)

(coordinate grid with points (6,4), (2,1), (8,1))

    b) **(0,4)**

Q2   The squares have sides of
        length 9 − 5 = 4.
        A: **(2,1)**
        B: **(10,9)**
        C: **(10,13)**

Q3   A **square** (rotated by 45°)

Activity:
e.g. (4,1), (5,2), (5,4), (4,7), (3,4) and
(3,2) are the vertices of a hexagon
with 1 line of symmetry.
(4,1), (5,2), (5,4), (4,5), (3,4) and
(3,2) are the vertices of a hexagon
with 2 lines of symmetry.

Answers

Page 101 — Drawing Shapes, Sheet 3

Q1 a) Horizontal lines go **across** the page.

b) Vertical lines go **up / down** the page.

Q2

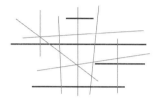

There are **4** horizontal lines.

Q3

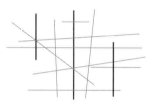

There are **3** vertical lines.

Activity:
The letters used should only be made up of horizontal and vertical lines.

Page 102 — Drawing Shapes, Sheet 4

Q1 Sets of lines **a)** and **e)** are parallel.

Q2 **C** and **E**

Q3

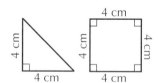

Measure the lengths of the sides and the angles in the drawings. Each side length should be correct to the nearest mm and each angle correct to the nearest degree.

Activity:
Make a plumb line and hang it next to things you think are vertical, if they are parallel to the string, they are vertical.

Page 103 — Drawing Shapes, Sheet 5

Q1

All the angles in the triangle should be 60°. All side lengths should be 3 cm.

Q2

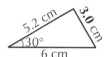

Each side length should be correct to the nearest mm and the 30° angle correct to the nearest degree.
The 3rd side is **30 mm** long

Q3

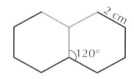

Activity:
After 90° the lines start spiralling outwards until you reach 180°. (After 180° they start spiralling in the other way.)

Page 104 — Symmetry, Sheet 3

Q1 Any 2 lines drawn through the circle are acceptable, and any 2 of the 5 lines of symmetry on the star are acceptable.

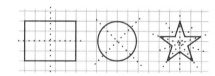

Q2

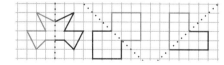

Q3

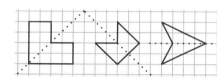

Activity:
For example:

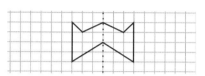

Page 105 — Symmetry, Sheet 4

Q1 Any 2 of these lines of symmetry:

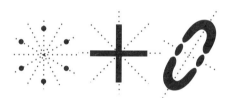

Q2

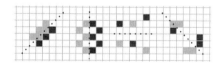

Q3

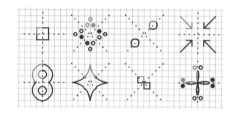

Activity:
For example, another pattern might be:

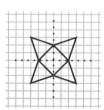

Answers

Page 106 — Symmetry, Sheet 5

Q1

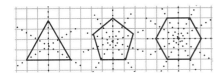

a) **Triangle (equilateral), 3 lines of symmetry.**
b) **Pentagon, 5 lines of symmetry.**
c) **Hexagon, 6 lines of symmetry.**

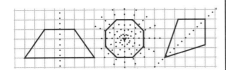

d) **Trapezium, 1 line of symmetry.**
e) **Octagon, 8 lines of symmetry.**
f) **Kite, 1 line of symmetry.**

Q2 Possible shapes might be:

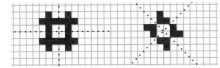

Activity:
For example, shapes with **3**, **4** and **5** lines of symmetry might look like:

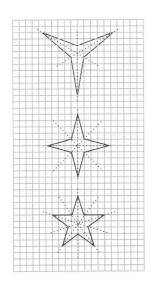

A shape with ten lines of symmetry might be a **decagon**:

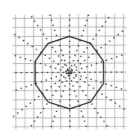

Page 107 — Transformations, Sheet 1

Q1 a)

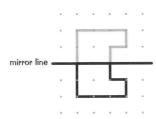

b)

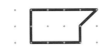

c)

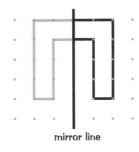

d)

Q2 a) and b)

Activity:
For example, using these two squares:

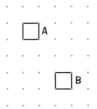

The instructions might be:
Translate A 2 units right and 3 units down.

Page 108 — Transformations, Sheet 2

Q1 a)

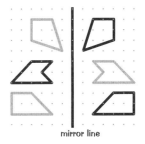

b)

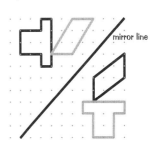

Q2 a) and b)

Answers

Activity:

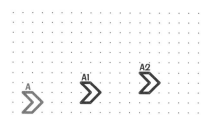

To translate A to A2:
Translate shape A 12 units right and 2 units up.
To translate A2 to A1:
Translate A2 6 units left and 1 unit down.

Page 109 —
Transformations, Sheet 3

Q1 a)

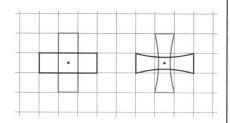

b)

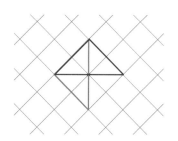

Q2

Q3 a), b) and c)

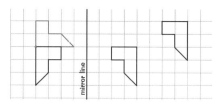

Activity:

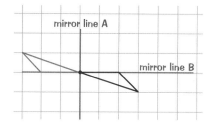

The same transformation could be done by mirroring the shape on line B, then mirroring it again on line A (or the other way round).
Yes, this will work for any shape.

Page 110 — Calculating
Perimeters and Areas,
Sheet 2

Q1 a) Several possible answers, e.g.

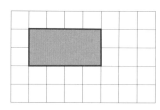

b) Several possible answers, e.g.

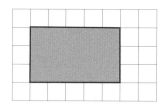

Q2 a) 30 + 40 + 30 + 40 = **140 cm**
    b) 90 + 50 + 90 + 50 = **280 cm**

Q3 a) **8 cm²**
    b) **10 cm²**
    c) **7 cm²**
    d) **11 cm²**

Activity:
Answer can be any three shapes as long as they have the same area.

Page 111 — Calculating
Perimeters and Areas,
Sheet 3

Q1 a) **10 cm**
    b) **12 cm**
    c) **12 cm**
    d) **14 cm**

Q2 a) **9 cm**
    b) **24 cm**
    c) **50 cm**
    d) **14 cm**

Q3 a) 4 cm × 3 cm = **12 cm²**
    b) 5 cm × 8 cm = **40 cm²**
    c) 9 cm × 7 cm = **63 cm²**
    d) 2 cm × 4 cm = **8 cm²**

Activity:
Many possible rectangles, e.g. length 4 cm, width 6 cm, or length 2 cm, width 8 cm.
The area will be different for each rectangle (unless any are congruent).

Page 112 — Calculating
Perimeters and Areas,
Sheet 4

Q1 a) perimeter = 12 + 12 + 6 + 6
        = **36 m**
        area = 12 × 6 = **72 m²**
    b) perimeter = 10 + 3 + 6 + 1 + 4 + 4 = **28 m**
        area = 10 × 3 + 4 × 1 = **34 m²**
    c) perimeter = 6 + 3 + 2 + 4 + 4 + 7 = **26 m**
        area = 6 × 3 + 4 × 4 = **34 m²**

Q2 a) **11 cm²**
    b) **12 cm²**
    c) **7 cm²**
    d) **12 cm²**

Activity:
Many possible answers depending on the length and width of the room.

Answers

Page 113 — Drawing and Measuring, Sheet 4

Q1 a) A 3 cm × 2 cm rectangle should be drawn.
Its perimeter is **10 cm.**

b) A 4 cm × 2 cm rectangle should be drawn.
Its perimeter is **12 cm.**

c) A 5 cm × 3 cm rectangle should be drawn.
Its perimeter is **16 cm.**

Q2 For each part, check that the rectangles have been drawn with the correct width and height.
The perimeters are:

a) **15 cm**

b) **17 cm**

c) **13 cm**

Activity
If the length and width of a rectangle add up to 10 cm, its perimeter will be 20 cm.
The possible rectangles are:

Length	Width
0.5 cm	9.5 cm
1 cm	9 cm
1.5 cm	8.5 cm
2 cm	8 cm
2.5 cm	7.5 cm
3 cm	7 cm
3.5 cm	6.5 cm
4 cm	6 cm
4.5 cm	5.5 cm
5 cm	5 cm

You can also swap the length and width of any of these rectangles.

Page 114 — Drawing and Measuring, Sheet 5

Q1 a) **44 mm**

b) Width = **38 mm**
Length = **22 mm**

c) **32 mm**

Q2 For parts a) – f) , check that the lines have been drawn with the correct length.

Q3 A rectangle of **width 30 mm** and **height 9 mm** should be drawn. The gap between each box should measure **4 mm**.

Activity
Many possible answers.

Page 115 — Drawing and Measuring, Sheet 6

Q1 a) The ends of snail A are at 23 mm and 72 mm.
Its length is
72 mm – 23 mm = **49 mm**.

b) The ends of snail B are at 47 mm and 81 mm.
Its length is
81 mm – 47 mm = 34 mm.
So snail A is
49 mm – 34 mm = **15 mm** longer than snail B.

c) Snail A's tail is at 23 mm.
Snail B's tail is at 47 mm.
The distance between their tails is 47 mm – 23 mm = **24 mm**

Q2 The distance between O and A is 30 mm.
The distance between O and B is 16 mm.
The distance between O and C is 24 mm.
The distance between A and B is 43 mm.
The distance between A and C is 44 mm.
The distance between B and C is 34 mm.

So:

b) OACB
= 30 mm + 44 mm + 34 mm
= **108 mm**

c) OBAC
= 16 mm + 43 mm + 44 mm
= **103 mm**

d) OBCA
= 16 mm + 34 mm + 44 mm
= **94 mm**

e) OCAB
= 24 mm + 44 mm + 43 mm
= **111 mm**

f) OCBA
= 24 mm + 34 mm + 43 mm
= **101 mm**

Activity
Many possible answers.
For a door measuring 75 cm × 195 cm, you could fit 97 postcards on to the door like this:

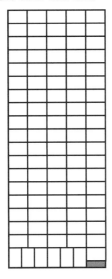

Page 116 — Reading Scales, Sheet 5

Q1 a) **36.4 °C**

b) **21.7 °C**

c) **23.6 °C**

d) **37.2 °C**

Q2 a) **250 ml**

b) **425 ml**

c) **3.5 litres**

d) **1.4 litres**

Q3 a) 70 – 55 = **15 kg**

b) 95 – 25 = **70 kg**

Activity:
The exact capacity readings will depend on the sizes of the yoghurt pots and other containers used.

Page 117 — Reading Scales, Sheet 6

Q1 a) **200, 450, 700**

b) **780, 805, 830**

c) **150, 250, 375**

d) **140, 180, 230**

e) **0.4, 1.8, 2.5, 3.6, 4.9**

f) **0.75, 2.5, 5.25**

g) **0.4, 1.2, 1.9, 2.7**

Answers

Q2 a) **600 ml**
b) **150 ml**
c) **7.5 litres**
d) **2.8 litres**

Activity:
A tape measure should be used to measure height, a set of scales to measure mass and a ruler (or tape measure) to measure handspan.

Page 118 — Reading Scales, Sheet 7

Q1 a) **2.5 °C**
b) **9 °C**
c) **3 °C**
d) **5 °C**
e) f)

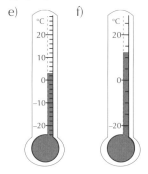

Q2 a) Bee Town = **10 miles**
Cockroach City = **20 miles**
Dragonfly City = **25 miles**
Earwig Town = **50 miles**
Flyville = **55 miles**
b)

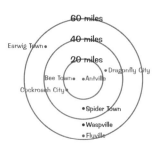

Activity:
A diagram with concentric circles and the home town marked in the centre should be produced.
The scale chosen will depend on the distances away of the places.
E.g. if the places chosen are all less than 20 miles away, 4 rings could be drawn and labelled 5 miles, 10 miles, 15 miles, 20 miles.

Page 119 — Reading Scales, Sheet 8

Q1   A = 125 g
B = 600 g
difference = 600 – 125
= **475 g**

Q2 a) **16 mm**
b) **2 cm**
c) toadstool = 2.1 cm
insect = 0.6 cm
difference = 2.1 – 0.6
= 1.5 cm = **150 mm**
d)

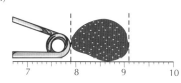

Q3 a)

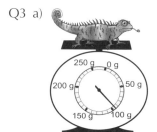

b)

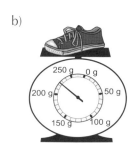

Activity:
E.g. melon = 220 g

Page 120 — Time, Sheet 3

Q1 b)

c)

d) **7:42 (accept 7:41-7:43)**

Q2 a) **12:10 pm**
b) **12:35 am**
c) **7:00 pm**

Q3 a) **27 days**
b) **54 seconds**

Q4 a) **2 hours 23 minutes** or **143 minutes**.
b) **45 minutes**

Activity:
For example, the places might be Sheffield and Birmingham.

If a train left Sheffield at 1:13 and got into Birmingham New Street at 2:26, the length of time the journey takes would be **1 hour 13 minutes** or **73 minutes**.

Page 121 — Time, Sheet 4

Q1 a) **16:45**
b) **18:15**

Q2 a) **11:50 pm**
b) **5:31 pm**
c) **12.11 am**

Q3 a) **7:00 until 9:30** and **12:00 until 17:30**.
b) **8 hours**
c) **19:01.** He will be late.

Activity:
For example, a film might start at **20:00**, last for **1 hour 45 minutes** and finish at **21:45**.

Answers

Page 122 — Time, Sheet 5

Q1 a) **16th August**
   b) **30th August**
   c) **14 days**

Q2 a) **Monday**
   b) **9th August**
   c) **14th August**

Q3 a) **Monday**
   b) **Friday**

Activity:
For example, the birthdays of two brothers might be **Wednesday, October 1st** and **Thursday, January 15th**.

There would be **106 days** between the two birthdays (or 259 going the other way).

Page 123 — Units and Measures, Sheet 5

Q1   metres: **3500**
      centimetres: **350 000**

Q2 a) **240 km**
   b) **140 g**
   c) **2.5 l**
   d) **250 cm**

Q3   **20 cm, 2 m, 250 cm, 2.6 m, 200 m, 2 km**

Q4 a) Length = **4.5 cm**
   b) Length = **7 cm**

Activity:
E.g. 9.6 cm would round to **9.5 cm**.

Page 124 — Units and Measures, Sheet 6

Q1   8.7 cm = **9 cm**

Q2   **Scale 3** should be ticked.

Q3   The vase can hold 2.8 ÷ 2 = 1.4 litres.
      It contains 1.4 ÷ 2 = 0.7 litres = **700 ml**

Activity:
E.g. if one apple weighs 90 g and the bag contains 8 apples, you could estimate that the bag of apples weighs **720 g**. It might actually weigh **750 g**. The estimate would be **30 g** different from the actual weight.

Page 125 — Units and Measures, Sheet 7

Q1 a) **0.8 kg**
   b) **200 g**
   c) **20 g**

Q2 a) **3600 g**
   b) **4500 g**
   c) **9900 g**

Q3 a) **Day 3**
   b) 1700 + 3800 + 4300 = **9800 m**

Activity:
E.g if the distance is 45 km, this is **45 000 m** and **4 500 000 cm**.

Page 126 — Units and Measures, Sheet 8

Q1 a) 1050 ÷ 150 = **7**
   b) 150 × 100 = 15 000 ml = **15 l**

Q2 a) **2.31 l**
   b) **6740 g**
   c) **1550 cm**
   d) **1.25 km**

Q3 a) **600 cm**
   b) 600 ÷ 120 = **5 times**
   c) 120 × 8 = 960 cm = **9.6 m**

Activity:
E.g. if the mug holds 300 ml, this is 0.3 litres.

Page 127 — Analysing Data, Sheet 1

Q1 a) **6**
   b) **5**
   c) **2**

Q2 a) **Penny**
   b) 48 + 67 + 134 + 121 + 15 = **385 coins**

Q3   **1901-1925**

Activity:
e.g.

Blue	Red	White	Green
15	27	8	5

2-brick	4-brick	6-brick	8-brick
11	8	22	14

The mode colour is red.
The mode size is a 6-brick.

Page 128 — Analysing Data, Sheet 2

Q1   **4**

Q2   Answers will vary. There should be more 9s than any other number, e.g. 1, 2, 3, 4, 5, 6, 9, 9.

Q3 a) 20 + 12 + 5 + 14 = 51
      54 − 51 = **3 bees**
   b) **Ants**

Q4 a) **£1.20**
   b) **Ninety-eight**

Activity:
e.g. 13 words per line
     4 letters per word

Page 129 — Analysing Data, Sheet 3

Q1 a) £20 + £50 + £20 + £40 + £60 + £70 + £20 = **£280**
   b) £280 ÷ 7 = **£40**
   c) £70 − £20 = **£50**

Q2 a) **1 hour**
   b) Put the times in order:
      1 hr, 1 hr, 2 hrs, 3 hrs, 5 hrs
      Median is the middle value:
      2 hours

Q3 a) 8.2 + 4.7 + 2.8 + 7.2 + 1.4 + 12.8 + 4.2 = 41.3
      41.3 ÷ 7 = **5.9**
   b) Put the numbers in order:
      1.4, 2.8, 4.2, 4.7, 7.2, 8.2, 12.8
      Median is the middle value:
      4.7
   c) 12.8 − 1.4 = **11.4**

Activity:
e.g. mean: 26.15
     median: 27
     range: 12

Answers

Page 130 — Chance and Likelihood, Sheet 1

Q1 a) **likely**
b) **certain**
c) **unlikely**
d) **unlikely**
e) **impossible**

Q2 **Three sections** of the spinner should be shaded.

Q3 One and six should **both** be underlined.
Odd number and even number should **both** be underlined.
Multiple of two should be underlined, but **not** multiple of three.

Activity:
e.g.
Certain:
If today is Monday, tomorrow will be Tuesday.
Impossible:
You roll a seven on an ordinary 6-sided dice.

Page 131 — Chance and Likelihood, Sheet 2

Q1 a) **black**
b) **White** and **striped** (since there are two of each).
c) **spotty**

Q2 a) **2** and **4**
b) Ryan is **correct**, since **more than half of the sections have a 6 in**.

Q3 A – **Even chance**
B – **Likely**
C – **Certain**
D – **Unlikely**

Activity:
a) You are **unlikely** to pick a queen.
b) You have an **equal chance** of picking a red card.

Page 132 — Chance and Likelihood, Sheet 3

Q1 The finished spinner should have **3 circles**, **3 triangles** and **2 squares**.

Q2 B – **answers will vary**
C – **even chance**
D – **impossible**
E – **about half way between "impossible" and "even chance"**

Q3 a) **False**
b) **True**
c) **True**

Activity:
For the spinners in question 3, you can have any score between 6 and 10. The most likely score is 8. The least likely score is 6.

Page 133 — Conclusions, Sheet 1

Q1 a) 3 boys and 3 girls.
6 people in total.
b) **yellow** and **green**
c) Kate is wrong because blue is the second most popular colour with girls. Only one fewer girls than boys chose it as their favourite colour.
d) Answers will vary.
E.g. Which colour is the least popular with boys?

Activity:
E.g. Young children prefer primary colours.
Older people prefer more muted colours.
Teenage girls like purple.

Page 134 — Conclusions, Sheet 2

Q1 a)

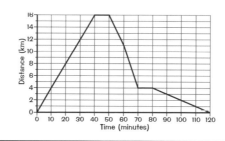

b) 30 minutes
c) He wasn't moving, so he could have been e.g. resting, eating, taking some photographs.
d) Answers will vary.
E.g. How far did Jonathan travel altogether?

Activity:
e.g. From a football league table you could answer the questions:
Which team has won the most matches this season?
Which team has lost the most matches this season?
Which team has the greatest goal difference?

Page 135 — Conclusions, Sheet 3

Q1 a) 77 °F, 25 °C
b) 0 °C, 32 °F
c) Convert the March New York temperature to °C:
41 °F = 5 °C.
5 °C – 5 °C = **0 °C**
d) No.
The lowest temperature in Manchester is 0 °C.
The lowest temperature in New York is 28 °F.
From the graph 28 °F < 0 °C.

Activity:
e.g.

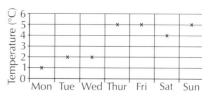

The temperature is higher in the second half of the week. At the start of the week, the sky was very clear. On Wednesday night, it clouded over and the temperature rose.

Page 136 — Data, Sheet 3

Q1 a) E.g. **What are your two favourite colours?**

b) E.g.

game	musical chairs	pass the parcel	Simon says	musical statues	blind man s buff
tally					
frequency					

c) E.g.
**Choose your favourite drink: cola, lemonade, juice
Choose your favourite sandwich: cheese, ham, egg
Choose your favourite sweet:
ice-cream, jelly, cake**

Activity:
E.g.

word	a	the	in	is	to	of
tally	III	IIII I	II	III	II	III

"**the**" is the most common word.

Page 137 — Data, Sheet 4

Q1 a)

Size	8	9	10	11	12	13	14
Tally	IIII II	IIII I	IIII	II	II	III	IIII
Frequency	7	6	5	2	2	3	4

b) **8**

Q2 E.g.
Record the colour of all the cars passing along a busy street for 10 minutes.
You could repeat the survey for a different street.

Activity:
E.g.

Score	1	2	3	4	5	6
Tally	IIII IIII	IIII III	IIII IIII	IIII III	IIII II	IIII II
Frequency	9	8	10	9	7	7

Each number comes up a similar number of times. (You can expect quite a bit of variation though.)

Page 138 — Data, Sheet 5

Q1 a) **Each person in Isaac's class could keep a TV diary. They would record how many hours of television they watch each day for a week.**

b)

Hours watched	0 to 3	3.5 to 6	6.5 to 9	9.5 to 12	12.5 to 15	15.5 to 18
Tally	I	III	IIII IIII	IIII II	IIII I	III
Frequency	1	3	10	7	6	3

c) **6.5 to 9 hours**

d) E.g.
Add up the total number of hours of television watched on each day and compare them.

Activity:
E.g.

Type of programme	soaps	comedy	sci-fi	reality	game shows
Tally	IIII	IIII I	III	IIII	IIII I
Frequency	5	6	3	4	6

Page 139 — Tables and Charts, Sheet 3

Q1 a)

Time	Tally	Total
9 am-10 am	IIII IIII IIII II	17
10 am-11 am	IIII III	8
11 am - 12 noon	II	2
12 noon - 1 pm	IIII IIII IIII IIII III	23
1 pm - 2 pm	IIII IIII IIII	14
2 pm - 3 pm	IIII IIII IIII	15
3 pm - 4 pm	IIII	5

b) **25**   c) **afternoon**

d)
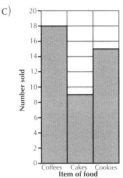

Q2 a) From bottom to top — **5, 10, 15, 20, 25, 30**

b) **A**

Activity:
A possible answer is:

Hearts	7
Clubs	10
Diamonds	7
Spades	6

Page 140 — Tables and Charts, Sheet 4

Q1 a) **7**
b) **36**
c)

Q2 a) **10**   b) **105**
c)

Mon	5
Tue	15
Wed	10
Thurs	25
Fri	20
Sat	30

Activity:
A possible answer is:

Cups	9
Plates	5
Bowls	6
Pans	6

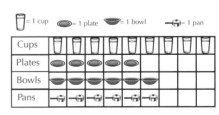

How many pans are there?
How many more bowls are there than plates?
Which item is there most of?

Answers

Page 141 — Tables and Charts, Sheet 5

Q1 a) **16 miles**   b) **40 miles**

Q2 a)

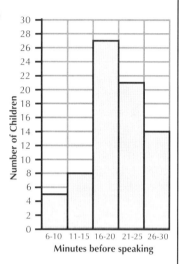

b) **35**

Q3 a) $\frac{1}{4}$

b) **3**

c) $\frac{3}{8}$

Activity:

A possible answer is:

Total	Frequency
2-5	7
6-8	14
9-12	9

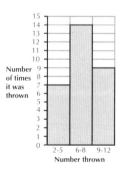

Name: .... Date: ....